Men-at-Arms • 551

Ottoman Armies 1820–1914

Gabriele Esposito • Illustrated by Giuseppe Rava

Series editors Martin Windrow & Nick Reynolds

OSPREY PUBLISHING
Bloomsbury Publishing Plc
Kemp House, Chawley Park, Cumnor Hill, Oxford OX2 9PH, UK
29 Earlsfort Terrace, Dublin 2, Ireland
1385 Broadway, 5th Floor, New York, NY 10018, USA
E-mail: info@ospreypublishing.com
www.ospreypublishing.com

OSPREY is a trademark of Osprey Publishing Ltd

First published in Great Britain in 2023

A catalogue record for this book is available from the British Library

ISBN: PB: 9781472855374; eBook: 9781472855381; ePDF: 9781472855398;
XML: 9781472855404

23 24 25 26 27   10 9 8 7 6 5 4 3 2 1

Editor: Martin Windrow
Index by Richard Munro
Typeset by PDQ Digital Media Solutions, Bungay, UK
Printed in India by Replika Press Private Ltd.

Osprey Publishing supports the Woodland Trust, the UK's leading woodland
conservation charity.

To find out more about our authors and books, visit **www.ospreypublishing.com**.
Here you will find extracts, author interviews, details of forthcoming events, and
the option to sign up for our newsletter.

Dedication

To my parents Maria Rosaria and Benedetto, whose advice is always precious
to me.

Acknowledgements

My thanks are due to the series editor, Martin Windrow, for supporting the idea
of this book from the beginning, and for his invaluable advice. Another special
acknowledgement goes to Giuseppe Rava for his magnificent colour plates,
which recreate the appearance and atmosphere of an almost forgotten
military world.
Most of the pictures published in this book are obtained from the Digital
Collections of the New York Public Library; the original files are available at:
https://digitalcollections.nypl.org/

Title Page

Detail from group photo of Ottoman troops at the time of the Crimean War,
1853-56. They include lancers of the 1st Cossack Regt, wearing Polish-style
uniform with frogged coats; for colours, see Plate D3. At right are a line of
infantryman and an artilleryman in Ottoman M1853 uniforms, the former with
white summer trousers and the latter with dark blue with red side-stripes. For
description, see commentary to Plate C1.

OPPOSITE
**Detail from a photo of Ottoman line infantry on parade
wearing the red *fez*, and M1879/93 dark blue uniforms with
red collars, shoulder straps, piping, cuff flaps and trouser
side-stripes; see Plate H1. These two junior NCOs display
inverted red rank chevrons on the upper left sleeve.**

OTTOMAN ARMIES 1820–1914

INTRODUCTION

During the 'long' 19th century the Ottoman Empire was called by the so-called Great Powers the 'sick man of Europe', as it was repeatedly and successfully challenged by both external enemies and internal insurgencies. Throughout this period Russia sought to expand its own empire at the Ottomans' expense, and Austria (from 1867, the Austro-Hungarian Empire) remained opportunistically hostile. Rebellions in the Ottomans' Balkan possessions successively achieved for them more autonomous status as vassal states, on their road to full independence. Meanwhile, both France and Britain intervened in Ottoman affairs – occasionally assisting the Empire simply in order to check Russian expansion, but more often supporting its vassals' struggles for self-determination. From the 1870s, Bismarck's Prussia also interfered diplomatically in order to thwart Russia.

At the turn of the 18th/19th centuries the multi-ethnic Empire which was nominally ruled from Istanbul had still been, on the map, extremely extensive. The Ottoman territories comprised Anatolia (modern Turkey), a large portion of the Middle East, most of the southern Balkans, the southern Caucasus, a number of eastern Mediterranean islands, the coastline of Arabia, and that of North Africa from Egypt right across to the eastern border of Morocco. However, the Empire remained essentially a medieval Islamic state, and its institutions were weakened by endemic corruption and nepotism. It was fragmented both politically and militarily, with the Sultans exerting direct control only over Anatolia, and self-seeking provincial governors wielding virtually independent powers further afield. Since the Ottomans had taken no part in the 18th-century revolution of military technology, organization and tactics, their armies were antiquated and most of the leaders stubbornly conservative. Against a background of chronically dwindling economic resources, it became increasingly clear that the Ottoman Turkish state had entered a long period of inexorable decline.

The first half of the 19th century saw the emergence of national consciousness in the Empire's various Balkan territories, and the Turks faced repeated revolts in Serbia/Bosnia, Montenegro, Greece,

Moldavia and Wallachia. The first three were garrisoned by Turkish troops, while the last two – the so-called 'Danubian Principalities' – were vassals, enjoying a degree of internal autonomy while still under Turkish taxation and theoretical rule. In North Africa the Ottomans maintained only limited numbers of troops in the major port-cities: Algiers, Tunis, Tripoli and Alexandria. The local governors of what are now Algeria, Tunisia and Libya (the latter comprising Tripolitania and Cyrenaica) paid the Turkish central authorities only nominal respect, ruling independently over piratical city-states. In Egypt, despite a Turkish garrison in Alexandria, the country was actually ruled by a powerful hereditary warrior class known as the Mamelukes. In the Middle East the Ottomans exerted more direct control over most of their territories, with the exception of Arabia; there, again, the Turkish presence was limited to coastal cities, while the vast interior was dominated by nomadic Arab tribes. In northern Mesopotamia and in the southern Caucasus some local peoples, such as the Kurds and Armenians, were also largely autonomous.

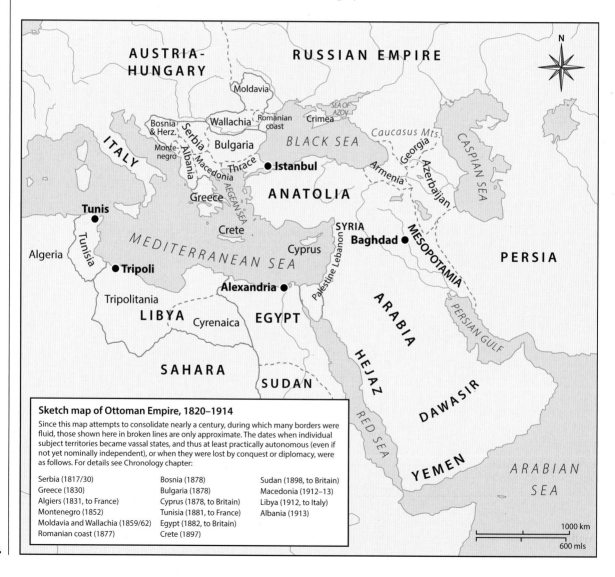

Sketch map of Ottoman Empire, 1820–1914

Since this map attempts to consolidate nearly a century, during which many borders were fluid, those shown here in broken lines are only approximate. The dates when individual subject territories became vassal states, and thus at least practically autonomous (even if not yet nominally independent), or when they were lost by conquest or diplomacy, were as follows. For details see Chronology chapter:

Serbia (1817/30)	Bosnia (1878)	Sudan (1898, to Britain)
Greece (1830)	Bulgaria (1878)	Macedonia (1912–13)
Algiers (1831, to France)	Cyprus (1878, to Britain)	Libya (1912, to Italy)
Montenegro (1852)	Tunisia (1881, to France)	Albania (1913)
Moldavia and Wallachia (1859/62)	Egypt (1882, to Britain)	
Romanian coast (1877)	Crete (1897)	

1000 km

600 mls

The 18th-century army

There were five main categories of troops. The regular, centrally-paid *kapikulu* were supported by semi-professional *toprakh* contingents hired by provincial governors. There were also three classes of militia: frontier *miri-askeris,* available only for short-term service, and urban *yerli nerefats* and rural *gonulluyan,* who could be mobilized only to face foreign invasions. The inadequacy of the regular forces led to a widespread reliance on mercenaries and locally-raised frontier troops, which further weakened Istanbul's military and therefore political control.

Mesopotamia (modern Iraq) was guarded by enforced converts from Georgia and Arab mercenaries. Syria provided very few troops, and relied upon mercenaries from North Africa, the Balkans and Anatolia. Lebanon raised two mutually hostile militias from the Druze and Christian communities, who frequently fought each other. Palestine raised a few local levies but mostly hired mercenaries, including Balkan cavalry.

The regulars, built around the Janissary infantry corps, were only a degenerate echo of their 16th-century glory days. The Janissaries were now a hereditary warrior caste, riddled with corruption, nepotism and absenteeism, whose officers routinely embezzled the wages of 'ghost' soldiers. They pursued political intrigues to preserve their many privileges, and their potential leadership of coups made them 'king-makers' in the manner of ancient Rome's Praetorian Guard. By the end of the century the original manpower of conscripted and converted Balkan youngsters had largely been replaced by Turkish volunteers. Both in Anatolia and the provinces the Janissaries included many self-seeking chancers who had joined simply to take advantage of the corps' status, paying *yamak* auxiliaries to perform their duties. Only a few units posted to far-flung provincial capitals maintained their military discipline and efficiency. Lowlier regulars who provided fortress garrisons were levied Anatolian *azaps,* Albanian Muslim mercenary *arnauts,* and provincially-hired *stratkulu* (who, nevertheless, included pioneers and miners to support the artillery).

Cavalry paid by the central government were the *kapikulu Sipahis,* backed on the frontiers by *Delis* irregulars. In Egypt the Mameluke heavy cavalry, originally Georgian and Circassian converts, had also degenerated into a self-interested caste who increasingly hired mercenaries and auxiliaries. The Ottoman artillery was weak, dispersed, and had no permanent organization, relying on hired foreign officers and Balkan mercenary gunners.

Between 1770 and 1795 several attempts were made to reform the regulars, but, since these necessarily involved eliminating corruption and dismissing incompetents, all were foiled by the traditionalist leaders of the Janissaries and *Sipahis.* However, a small modernized Rapid-Fire Artillery Corps *(Suratçi Ocagi)* was created, and new technical schools gave birth to engineer, pontoon and artillery wagon units.

Egyptian Mameluke, early 19th century; the dress of the Ottoman *Sipahis* was not dissimilar, consisting of a turban and multi-coloured garments often made of silk. The main weapon of both Mamelukes and *Sipahis* at this period was a lance, but they also carried a sabre, at least a couple of flintlock pistols, and curved daggers.

Both figures date from 1818, and wear traditional dress. (Left) Officer of a *toprakh* regional contingent: white turban; red jacket with yellow frogging; very loose light blue trousers, and brown leather boots. He carries four flintlock pistols tucked into the waist-sash, and a small horn for transmitting orders. (Right) Gunner of the *Topçu Ocagi* artillery corps: black-striped yellow turban wrapped around red cap; medium blue cloak adorned with tasselled white 'loops'; red jacket, very loose green trousers, and red boots. The gun is a pre-Napoleonic piece, locally produced in Istanbul.

The first 'westernized' dress worn by the *Nizam-i Cedit*, 1805. (Left) This fusilier of the 2nd Inf Regt is uniformed similarly to Plate A1, but entirely in dark blue; the European officer instructor (right) has a dark blue cap and coat, grey trousers and a red sash.

The 'New Army', 1794–1807

Attempts at military reform were repeated during this period, but were again defeated by the traditional leadership class.

Impressed by a Russian bodyguard raised by the Grand Admiral of the Ottoman Navy in 1791, Sultan Selim III (r. 1789–1807) decided in 1794 to create a New Army *(Nizam-i Cedit)*, disciplined, trained, armed and uniformed along Western lines. An embryo *Bostanci* musketeer regiment was raised within his Imperial Guard, and by 1797 this had three *tabor* battalions each with 12 *boluk* companies and an additional one-gun artillery section. Following Napoleon's invasion of Egypt the sultan enlarged this corps, with French instructors replacing the original Russians. By the end of 1805 the mostly Anatolian *Nizam-i Cedit* had 26,000 men in 12 two-battalion infantry regiments and one 10-battery artillery regiment. Foreign observers were complimentary about the New Army, and some units would earn respect in battle against the First Serbian Uprising and at Gaza and Acre.

The entrenched conservative leadership were deeply hostile to the sultan's initiative, and when the New Army tried to recruit in the Balkans an armed confrontation broke out in Bulgaria and Thrace in 1806. This so-called 'Edirne incident' saw *Nizam-i Cedit* troops defeated by a traditionalist force; in 1807 Selim III was deposed and assassinated by a Janissary uprising, and the New Army was disbanded (though its artillery survived). Supporters of Selim's policies included Alemdar Mustafa Pasha, grand vizier of the new Sultan Mustafa IV (r. 1807–08). This chief minister tried to assemble *Nizam-i Cedit* veterans into a new force under a 'false flag' Janissary title, but he was killed during a second Janissary mutiny.

The Empire during the Napoleonic Wars

The Ottoman Empire played only a marginal role in the Napoleonic Wars, which nevertheless disrupted it badly, and a number of Turkish military humiliations were inflicted by both sides as the weak Empire tried to manoeuvre for advantage during the successive coalitions against Napoleon.

In Egypt, the French and subsequent British invasions led to the complete defeat of the Mamelukes, and their replacement from 1803 by a mutinous Ottoman army of Albanian *arnaut* mercenaries led by one Muhammad Ali, who had virtually seceded from the Empire by the time he defeated a second British expedition in 1807. Sultan Mustafa IV survived only 14 months before being deposed and killed by his half-brother Mahmud II in November 1808. During 1807–09 the Turks had an alliance with France, but were then forced by Britain to renounce it. Nevertheless, until 1812 the Empire was also at war with Russia over the Danubian Principalities; in that year the Treaty of Bucharest forced them to hand over eastern Moldavia and to recognize the autonomy of Wallachia and western Moldavia under Russian influence. During 1807–12, another Russian army also attacked the Ottomans in the Caucasus.

Officer of *Nizam-i Cedit* 1st Inf Regt, 1807, in the same uniform colours as Plate A1. His status is displayed by gold embroidery on his cuffs and the neck and front of his jacket, and by a brass badge on his headgear.

Meanwhile, in 1804 the first major 'national' uprising of the Serbs took place; although supported by the Russians from 1807, it ended indecisively in 1813. During 1815–17, however, a second Serbian rebellion finally achieved autonomous vassal status for their country, which by 1826 was well established and had its own small army. The years 1798–1815 also saw the outbreak of several local uprisings in Greece, with limited support from the British, which were crushed only with difficulty.

During these turbulent years the Ottoman Empire also had to face a major rebellion in Arabia, which was inspired by the reformist Wahhabi religious movement and led, in part, by Abdullah bin Saud. The Arab rebels declared their own nomadic 'Emirate of Diriyah' in central Arabia, and launched large-scale incursions into Ottoman territories in Iraq. Unable to defeat them, the Ottomans had no choice but to make peace with Muhammad Ali of Egypt in return for him agreeing to send troops to crush the Arabian revolt. This conflict of 1811–18 ended with Egyptian victory, further cementing Muhammad Ali's power in the Middle East.

CHRONOLOGY, 1815–1914

1815: In Mani peninsula of the southern Peloponnese, Ottoman expeditionary force is defeated by Greek guerrillas fighting for national independence. Meanwhile, in the northern Balkans, Second Serbian Uprising begins: the Serbians, backed by Russia and Austria, fight to re-establish their autonomous vassal status. In North Africa, a US naval squadron fights its way into port of Algiers and enforces right of peaceful passage for US shipping in the Mediterranean.

1816: Joint Anglo-Dutch fleet bombards Algiers, and frees many Christian slaves. Meanwhile, the Ottomans continue to fight the Serbian rebels, and their Egyptian allies make progress against the Arabian insurgents.

1817: Second Serbian Uprising ends in victory, and Principality of Serbia is established as an autonomous vassal state of the Ottoman Empire.

1818: Victory over the Wahhabis leads to deployment of Egyptian garrisons in strategic locations in Arabia.

1821: Major uprising against a pro-Turkish regime breaks out in Wallachia, with help from Greek expatriates. After some early victories the insurgents are defeated; meanwhile, guerrillas in central Greece and the Peloponnese also harass Turkish garrisons.The Ottomans also begin a war against Persia for control of Azerbaijan on their north-east border, but their army is badly defeated at Erzurum.

1822–23: Fragmented Greek revolution spreads throughout the country, from Macedonia to the islands of Crete and Cyprus. Greek national assembly proclaims independence and writes the first constitution. Meanwhile, the Ottoman-Persian War comes to an indecisive end.

1824–26: The Turks request Egyptian help against Greek rebels. Muhammad Ali sends his navy and a large 'semi-westernized' expeditionary force to the Aegean, and soon wins several victories over the insurgents.

1827: Britain, France and Russia send naval forces to the Aegean and provide the Greek rebels with substantial military supplies. On 20 October 1827 their joint fleet defeats the Ottoman-Egyptian-Tunisian navy at the battle of Navarino. Thereafter, the Ottomans are obliged to adopt a defensive stance in Greece.

1828–29: A French expeditionary force lands in southern Greece to support local rebels. After suffering several more defeats, Muhammad Ali evacuates Egyptian troops. For lack of military resources, the Ottomans have no choice but to accept Greece's *de facto* independence. Meanwhile, in June 1828 in the northern Balkans, a large Russian army crosses the Danube and quickly occupies the Danubian Principalities.

1829: Despite a series of victories, the Russian advance towards Anatolia is blocked by Turkish fortifications in Bulgaria. This Russo–Turkish war ends on 14 September 1829 with the Treaty of Adrianople: the Ottoman Empire cedes to Russia territory on the Black Sea coast and in Armenia; Moldavia and Wallachia become Russian protectorates with their own small armies; and the practical autonomy of the Principality of Serbia is confirmed.

1830: Under strong pressure from Britain, France and Russia, the Ottoman Empire is forced to formally recognize Greek independence. During the same year, on 14 June, a large French punitive force lands at Algiers. The local Ottoman garrison is defeated within days, and the Empire abandons the Arab and Berber tribes of the hinterland to their own devices.

1831–33: Despite several victories, a major revolt in Bosnia is finally crushed by Turkish troops at Sarajevo in 1832. Meanwhile, Egypt and the Ottoman Empire fight a major war. Muhammad Ali's son, Ibrahim Pasha, invades Palestine and Syria and captures Aleppo, Homs, Beirut, Sidon, (Syrian) Tripoli and Damascus. The modernized Egyptian army advances into central Anatolia before a Russian intervention ends the conflict. Egypt nominally remains a vassal state, but now controls Palestine, Syria and Arabia.

1833: Revolts in Albania are suppressed.

1834–38: Further Balkan guerrilla uprisings, mainly in southern Albania, cause heavy Ottoman losses, but another in Tripolitania achieves little. Meanwhile, Ibrahim Pasha crushes revolts in Palestine and Syria, and by the Druzes in Lebanon.

1839–41: Ottoman attempt to reconquer Syrian territory ceded to Ibrahim Pasha starts second major Turkish-Egyptian war. The Turkish advance is defeated at Nezib on 24 June 1839, but the consequent Egyptian threat to Anatolia itself is averted by British, Russian and Austrian naval blockades, bombardments and landings. Under their pressure, Egypt is forced to return all Ottoman territories captured over the previous decade.

1843–62: Revolts in different areas of the Empire. Albanian rebels achieve little during 1843–44. In 1848 Moldavia and Wallachia attempt to gain independence from both Russia and Turkey, but Russian influence is restored after a few months. In 1852, both the Montenegrins and the Serbs of Herzegovina rebel against the Turks. The Montenegrins are successful, forming the vassal Principality of Montenegro, but, despite dragging on until 1862, the Serbian rising in Herzegovina is finally suppressed.

1853–56: Crimean War. Following a new Russian invasion of the Danubian Principalities, Britain and France (and later the Italian kingdom of Piedmont/Sardinia) side with the Ottomans in order to halt Russian expansion. The Turks are successful in the Balkans, but also have to fight a Russian army in the Caucasus, and rebellious Greeks in Epirus (north-west Greece/southern Albania). Crimean War ends with Treaty of Paris (30 March 1856), limiting Russian activity in Black Sea. The status quo is restored in the Balkans, but the Danubian Principalities (temporarily occupied by 'neutral' Austria during the Crimean War) become practically independent.

1858–62: New conflict between Ottoman Empire and Montenegro; after a short campaign the Turks are defeated at Grahovacs, and Montenegro preserves its autonomy. In

1859 the Danubian Principalities are unified into what later becomes the independent Kingdom of Romania. In 1860 a bloody civil war breaks out in Lebanon between Druzes and Christians. Napoleon III of France sends an expeditionary corps, which obliges Ottoman troops to disarm the Druzes. During 1861–62 the Montenegrins try to expand their territory into Herzegovina, but without success.

1866–69: An uprising in Crete is crushed by an Egyptian expeditionary force.

1875–76: Herzegovina and Bulgaria rebel against the Empire without success. In 1876, both Serbia and Montenegro declare war on the Ottomans, and an uprising in Bulgaria leads to reports of Turkish atrocities which cause outrage in Europe.

1877–78: The Russo–Turkish War breaks out in April 1877, when Russian armies cross the Danube and march south to support the Serbian-Montenegrin alliance. This is soon also joined by Romania, and an anti-Turkish uprising also breaks out in Epirus. Russia wins decisive victory by February 1878, and obtains much territory under the Treaty of Santo Stefano (3 March). Bulgaria becomes an autonomous vassal, and Montenegro, Serbia and Romania become independent nations. This settlement is rejected by the Great Powers at the Congress of Berlin in June-July. While Bosnia-Herzegovina resists Austro-Hungarian occupation, a revised settlement (13 July 1878) reduces Russian and Bulgarian gains, thus ensuring simmering resentments that will lead to the Balkan Wars in 1912–13.

1893–96: The Ottoman Empire is torn by another series of internal revolts, in Qatar (1893), Armenia (1894–96), and Macedonia. Supported by several of the new Balkan nations, Macedonian guerrillas fight the Turks from 1893 to 1908.

1897: A Greco-Turkish war is fought for possession of the island of Crete. While the Empire is militarily victorious, it is forced by the Great Powers to grant Crete autonomous status.

1908: The so-called 'Revolution of the Young Turks'. Impelled by officers of the Ottoman army, this political movement – the Committee of Union and Progress – forces Sultan Abdul Hamid II to agree to a constitution allowing free political parties. Exploiting the turmoil, Greece annexes Crete, and the Austro-Hungarians annex Bosnia-Herzegovina.

1909–10: The Ottoman army crushes limited but bloody rebellions in both Lebanon and Albania.

1911–12: The Italian-Turkish War. The Kingdom of Italy invades weakly-defended Ottoman Libya, and mounts naval attacks in the Aegean Sea. By the Treaty of Lausanne (18 October 1912) the Turks cede Libya to Italy, which also occupies the Greek islands of the Dodecanese.

1912–13: First Balkan War (8 October 1912–30 May 1913). The 'Balkan League' (Greece, Serbia, Montenegro and Bulgaria) expel Ottoman forces from the Balkans. Ruling 'Young Turks' triumvirate under Ismail Enver Pasha rejects draft peace terms. Further Balkan League victories lead to Treaty of London (30 May).

1913: Second Balkan War (30 June–30 July 1913). Bulgaria, dissatisfied with its gains in Macedonia, attacks Greek and Serbian forces, who are supported by Romania and Montenegro; the Ottomans also take the opportunity to recapture eastern Thrace. Quickly defeated, Bulgaria loses most of its gains from the First War; Macedonia is divided, and Albania becomes an independent nation under the protection of the Great Powers. Strong German military mission arrives in Istanbul in December, and is given widespread authority.

1914: Ottoman Empire enters World War I (29 October) on the side of the Central Powers – Germany and Austria-Hungary.

An Albanian *arnaut* mercenary, *c.*1830; until the Crimean War most Albanian mercenaries in Ottoman or Egyptian service dressed in this manner. This image shows a black-tasselled red *fez*; an emerald-green jacket with red collar-edging and shoulder-rolls; a white *fustanella* kilt, and green leggings with black trim.

REFORMS UNDER MAHMUD II, 1826–39

Disbandment of the Janissaries

Given the turmoil of 1807–08, the new Sultan Mahmud II (r. 1808–39) at first had no choice but to indulge the most conservative elements of his forces, but over time it became apparent that the Empire's military situation was unsustainable. The steady modernization of Muhammad Ali's Egyptian army in the 1820s would soon make it the dominant military machine in the Middle East. The Ottoman armies had performed badly against both the Arabian Wahhabis and the Greek insurgents in the southern Balkans, to the point that the sultan had no choice but to request Egyptian military assistance. In about 1825 Mahmud II recognized that a general reform of his armed forces could no longer be postponed – and that this would only be possible if he freed himself from the Janissaries.

To achieve this, Mahmud made a secret agreement with the Janissaries' long-time rivals for influence and privileges, the cavalry *Sipahis*. In the early months of 1826 the sultan announced that he was going to organize a new army structured and trained along modern European lines. Predictably, on 14/15 June the Janissaries advanced on Mahmud's palace to depose him – only to be defeated by charging *Sipahis,* supported by the Sultan's modern artillery. Some 4,000 were killed over several days of street fighting; the rest fled the capital or were captured and executed, and Mahmud II officially disbanded the corps and confiscated their wealth. Following this so-called 'Auspicious Incident', the *Sipahis* briefly increased their own political power, but by 1828 the Sultan had made enough progress in organizing his 'westernized' force that he was able to revoke their privileges and disband them without resistance, absorbing the younger men into his new army.

Rebirth of the New Army

The Imperial Guard was reorganized, with two 3-battalion *Bostansyan-i Hassa* infantry regiments, each 900-strong battalion having 9 companies. The most loyal of the former *Sipahis* formed a Guard lancer regiment of three 150-man squadrons. Additionally, selected former Janissaries were organized as a ceremonial Halberdier bodyguard company.

The reformed Ottoman 'line' army was soon given the revived title of *Nizam-i Cedit.* Many European veterans of the Napoleonic Wars formed the instructional backbone of the new units, achieving significant improvements over only a few years. The first branch to be modernized was the infantry, under the overall command of a single *bash-bimbashi,* with a *topchi-bashi* in command of the integral light artillery detachments. In 1828 there were 33 line regiments or *alays,* each commanded by a *miralay* (colonel), supported by a lieutenant-colonel and a quartermaster. The regiment's

Imperial Guard infantryman (left) and line infantryman (right) of the *Nizam-i Cedit* in M1826 uniform. The guardsman wears a red *Bostanci* cap with yellow stripes, a red jacket and dark blue trousers. The line soldier has a yellow-striped dark blue *tarboosh,* a dark blue jacket bearing a white crescent on the chest, and dark blue trousers; both men wear black half-boots.

three small *tabor* battalions were each commanded by a *bimbashi* (major), supported by two adjutant-majors, one *sanjaqdar* standard-bearer and a secretary. A battalion consisted of just three 100-man *safs* (companies), each led by a *youzbashi* (captain) and two *moulazim* (lieutenants), with one sergeant-major, four senior and one junior sergeants. The detachments of 'cannon infantry' in each battalion were now assembled to form a single 120-man regimental company with 10 light guns. By the outbreak of the hostilities with Russia in 1828, the 33 line infantry regiments could in theory be grouped into *liwas* (brigades) and *hassas* (divisions). Most infantrymen were armed with French M1777 flintlock muskets or equivalent weapons.

While also reorganized, the New Army's cavalry and artillery remained of limited size. The first cavalry unit of the *Nizam-i Cedit* to be formed was the Christian so-called Silistra Cavalry Regt, raised in 1826 in the area around the Danube delta from the local Zaporozhian Cossacks. The regiment was organized in two battalions, the first of which was entirely equipped with lances. Soon afterwards two regiments of dragoons (armed with French flintlock carbines) were organized, each structured in six 150-man squadrons. By 1828 this internal organization had also been adopted by the Silistra regiment, which was renamed the Sesiasker Cavalry Regiment.

The Ottoman artillery was reorganized in 50 foot and 8 mounted batteries, each of which had a 100-man company strength. The foot batteries had 6-pdr, 8-pdr or 12-pdr guns, or alternatively heavy 24-pdr ox-drawn siege guns. The horse batteries and the 'cannon infantry' companies had light 3-pdr guns. No artillery battalions or regiments were formed, but in 1828–29 there was a *Humbaraci Ocagi* 'Regiment of Bombardiers', including many Polish military refugees, which was tasked with manufacturing, transporting and firing mortars, as well as mines and grenades, for siege operations. Additionally, a 1,250-strong 'Regiment of Miners' provided combat engineers and sappers.

The 35,000-strong New Army was still a work-in-progress when war with Russia broke out in 1828. Nearly wiped out during this disastrous conflict, from 1829 it had to be rebuilt almost from scratch.

Reconstruction and reserves, 1829–36

By the end of this difficult process the New Army consisted of the following units: 6 regiments of Guard infantry, 20 regiments of line infantry, 20 battalions of 'provincial' infantry; 3 regiments of Guard cavalry, 2 regiments of line cavalry, and an artillery corps.

Apparently the four new Guard infantry regiments were formed with survivors of pre-1828 line units, while the 20 line regiments were newly raised. The provincial infantry were the first embryonic form of a 'reserve army', mostly raised from militiamen in Thrace and western Anatolia. The three pre-1828 squadrons of Guard cavalry were transformed into

Officer (left) and fusilier of the 'cannon infantry', *c.*1830; both wear dark blue uniforms, the former with a brass plate applied to the chest and the latter with a white crescent. The officer's headgear and sash are red. The gunner's 'top hat' is black with a red top band and black tassel, and fur trim around the base.

regiments. The Sesiasker Cav Regt was disbanded after its recruiting area was ceded to Russia in 1829, so of the line cavalry only the two dragoon regiments remained. The artillery consisted of a variable number of independent companies, the regiments of bombardiers and of miners both having been disbanded. In 1834, after having restructured his forces, the sultan created a new military academy to train officers, in conjunction with the two existing technical schools. In 1836 the provincial units were organized for the first time as the *Redif* (reserve); while the active army was all-volunteer, this reserve was made up of former soldiers who could be conscripted for further service at need.

By 1837 the *Nizam-i Cedit* included the following units: 2 regiments of Guard infantry, 23 regiments of line infantry; 2 regiments of Guard cavalry, 4 regiments of line cavalry; 3 regiments of artillery and a regiment of engineers, plus an army reserve of 40 infantry battalions and 80 cavalry squadrons. All infantry regiments had four battalions, but their 'cannon infantry' were detached to form the three new 12-battery artillery regiments, which had an assortment of light, medium and heavy guns. The units of Guard cavalry were only 'paper' regiments, having only one lancer squadron each, while the four regiments of line cavalry were all carbine-equipped dragoons.

Albanian mercenaries, *c.*1835; note (left) characteristic winter cloak of raw white wool, and long tobacco pipe. Both wear soft red caps and white shirts and *fustanella* kilts. Typically the other garments, including the leggings, were heavily embroidered in decorative colours. Weapons were long flintlock hunting guns (note the oriental shape of the butt), pistols and daggers.

THE *TANZIMAT*, 1840–53

In 1839 Mahmud II died and was succeeded on the throne by Abdulmejid I. This great reforming sultan presided over an era of modernization that became known as the *Tanzimat* ('Reorganization'). His main aim was to secure the territorial integrity of the Ottoman Empire against both external aggression and internal nationalist movements. During his long reign (1839–61) Abdulmejid carried out several important institutional reforms, of which one was the introduction of military conscription.

Military regions and army corps

The war with Egypt in 1839-41 demonstrated that the *Nizam-i Cedit* was still too small and too concentrated around Istanbul to provide an effective defence of the Empire. In 1843 the army was greatly expanded, and the territory of the Empire was divided into five military regions, each of which was to be garrisoned by an army corps. The 1st or Imperial Guard Corps was headquartered at Istanbul, the 2nd Army Corps at Scutari (Albania), the 3rd at Monastir (Macedonia), the 4th at Kharpout (Anatolia), and the 5th at Damascus (Syria). The 1st and 3rd Army Corps each consisted of 7 three-battalion infantry regiments, 4 light infantry battalions, 5 cavalry regiments, and 1 regiment of artillery; two of the 1st Army Corps infantry regiments and two of its cavalry regiments were Imperial Guard units. The 2nd, 4th and 5th Army Corps each had 6 line infantry regiments, 6 light infantry battalions, 4 cavalry regiments and 1 of artillery. The whole Ottoman army thus comprised 32 line infantry regiments, 26 light infantry battalions, 22 cavalry regiments, and 5 artillery regiments.

An important innovation introduced by the reorganization of 1843 was the light infantry or *seshaneci* ('foot chasseurs', later 'rifles'). Until then Ottoman light infantry had been entirely made up of irregular mercenaries (*bashi-bazouks*) recruited from different areas of the Empire. The battalions of *seshaneci* were formed by selecting one-in-eight of the most agile and skilled soldiers from each line battalion. Equipped with flintlock carbines, they were trained to operate in broken terrain, with a higher degree of flexibility than the line infantry.

Of the cavalry, the two Imperial Guard units assigned to the 1st Army Corps were known, from the distinctive colours of their uniforms, as the 1st or Red Regt and the 2nd or Blue Regiment. The line cavalry regiments were all organized in six squadrons, the first two of each being equipped with carbines and the remaining four with lances. The only exception to this rule was the separate elite Guard 1st Lancer Regt, whose squadrons were all armed with lances.

Each of the artillery regiments consisted of 11 field companies/batteries each with 6 field guns, and one mountain company serving 4 mountain guns. In addition to the units deployed to the various Army Corps, the newly-created Grand Master of the Artillery commanded a reserve that was available for use all over the Empire: one additional 12-company field regiment, one 12-company regiment of fortress artillery, and two 2-battalion regiments of engineers which could be grouped into a single brigade.

Imperial Guard infantryman wearing M1839 uniform. The red *fez* has a dark blue tassel; the dark blue shell jacket has red facings at collar and cuffs, and (crudely rendered here) three tasselled red buttonhole loops across the chest. The dark blue trousers have red side-stripes, and note the pointed black shoes.

Conscription

The *Redif*, being formed of reservists who normally served for only one month each year, had a territorial organization. Each district of the Empire was to provide a four-battalion regiment of reserve infantry, and from one to four squadrons of reserve cavalry, depending upon its population.

In 1848 the first conscription law was proclaimed: each conscript (selected by lot) was to serve for 5 years in the *Nizam-i Cedit* and for 7 years in the *Redif* (although Christians and the inhabitants of Istanbul were both exempted). Also during 1848, a 7th Army Corps was created; based in Iraq, this consisted of 4 line infantry regiments, 4 light infantry battalions, 2 cavalry regiments and 1 of artillery.

Over the next few years the internal organization of units underwent some minor changes, usually involving enlargements to unit staffs. In order to develop stronger *esprit de corps*, all regiments received a band with 80 musicians. From 1846, Abdulmejid worked hard to improve the quality of the officer corps, fixing standards for the military academy and creating four new military colleges. He also established the Council of the Grand Master of the Artillery, divided into a War Dept and a Testing Department.

In 1848 the cavalry was expanded by the formation of two new regiments, both attached to the 3rd Army Corps: the Cossack Regt, and the Mounted Chasseurs Regiment. The first, recruited from Polish exiles and Zaporozhian Cossacks, was short-lived. The latter survived until the outbreak of the Crimean War; equipped entirely with carbines, it too was largely raised from Polish expatriates.

There were also a small naval infantry corps, and a large Gendarmerie corps. Abdelmejid reorganized the former as a single battalion of 500 men known as *galeonjis*, which always remained part of the Navy. The gendarmes or *zaptiye*, created in 1846, were paramilitary mounted police. Each *eyalet* or region of the Empire had a brigade of gendarmerie, Istanbul itself having three brigades. Each province had a company of *zaptiye*, dispersed in smaller detachments. In times of war a good number of these 30,000 Turkish mounted policemen could be mobilized, and brigaded to form an effective cavalry force.

THE CRIMEAN WAR, 1853–56

Ottoman campaigns

The dismissive allied comments about Ottoman troops at Balaclava do the army less than justice. The war began in late June 1853, when two Russian armies crossed into Moldavia and Wallachia and advanced to the Danube. The Ottoman general Omar Pasha defeated them in several actions between October 1853 and January 1854, and on 28 March 1854 Britain and France declared war on Russia. Russian sieges of Calafat and Silistra had to be abandoned in May and June, partly due to Austrian attacks on Russian supply lines, and by July 1854 – when the Anglo-French expeditionary forces reached Varna on the west coast of the Black Sea, preparatory to landing on the Crimean Peninsula in September – Omar Pasha had advanced far enough to threaten Bucharest. On 26 July the Tsar ordered a complete Russian retreat from the Danubian Principalities.

Ottoman regular soldiers wearing the new M1853 uniforms. (Foreground, left to right): line cavalry trooper; line cavalry officer, wearing non-regulation frogged and fur-trimmed 'patrol jacket'; line infantryman, and foot artilleryman, both wearing white summer trousers. For colours, see commentaries to Plates C1 and C2.

The other purely Ottoman campaign of the war was fought in the Caucasus, but this was a secondary and less impressive effort, notable for massive losses to disease. After a Turkish advance in October/November 1853 was checked, a seven-month stalemate ensued before a further series of Ottoman attempts and defeats. The Russians besieged the fortress of Kars from May to December 1855, when the Ottoman garrison surrendered. Omar Pasha had led a Turkish landing at Batoum on the Georgian coast in September 1855; intended to distract the Russians from the siege of Kars, it failed to achieve this. The fighting in this theatre ended indecisively.

Bashi-bazouks under European command

When hostilities commenced the *Nizam-i Cedit* was greatly outnumbered by the Russian armies, and was obliged to recruit large numbers of irregulars from the Empire's various ethnic groups, particularly Albanians and Circassians. These notoriously undisciplined *bashi-bazouks* ('crazy heads') were raised only in wartime, serving under their own chiefs and receiving no equipment or pay from the government. They were therefore motivated purely by the hope of plunder, and were infamous for cruelly preying upon civilian communities. Most fought on foot, but a certain number were fast-moving light horsemen.

British officer of Beatson's Horse, wearing a white turban wrapped around a peaked forage cap. For uniform colours, see Plate D2.

After arriving in the Ottoman Empire, both the allied British and French expeditions attempted to 'regularize' some of the large numbers of *bashi-bazouks* who had answered the call, proposing to the Ottoman authorities that officers and NCOs of their expeditionary forces should replace the *bashi-bazouks'* local chiefs or *sergerdes*. Both armies seem to have placed too much confidence in their previous success in forming native units in their own Indian and North African possessions. The French assembled a good number of mounted *bashi-bazouks* from Syria and Kurdistan, and on 24 June 1854 founded a corps of *Spahis d'Orient*, commanded by Gen Youssouf. He began to organize six regiments, each with one squadron of Syrians, one of Albanians, one of Kurds, and one of Turkomans. However, most of them deserted as soon as they had received new French weapons, and the *Spahis d'Orient* were disbanded in August 1854 before seeing any action.

The British made their own parallel attempt, under the command of Maj William Ferguson Beatson of the East India Company's Bengal army. With some other capable officers, Beatson (later known as 'Shemshi Pasha') recruited a total of some 4,000 irregulars. Paid by the British, and divided into five regiments under small British cadres, Beatson's Horse were ready to fight by the end of 1854. However, the British C-in-C Lord Raglan was never convinced of their value, and never authorized their deployment. After episodes of indiscipline due to a chronic lack of funds, in September 1855 Beatson's Horse was finally disbanded. Some of the best elements were quickly re-enlisted to form a new Osmanli Irregular Cavalry, but this was never properly organized, and was disbanded in its turn in July 1856 without having seen much fighting.

The Anglo–Turkish Contingent

The British recognized that Turkish infantrymen had great potential if they could be given capable junior leaders. The Ottoman authorities agreed to their organizing a large 'westernized' Anglo–Turkish Contingent of Turkish infantry under British cadres. Grudgingly, they even agreed to transfer some entire Ottoman regiments, purged of incompetent officers and sergeants. By August 1855 the ATC consisted of 10 regiments of line infantry, 2 cavalry regiments, and 4 artillery batteries; of these, 7 of the infantry regiments, both cavalry units and one battery came from the *Redif* rather than the active army.

After a few months the Anglo–Turkish Contingent received its definitive organization. It was now to consist of 16 line infantry regiments grouped in four 4-regiment brigades; 3 cavalry regiments; 6 batteries of foot artillery and 1 each of horse and garrison artillery; an engineer corps (including a small telegraph detachment), and a transport corps. Most of the officers for these units came from the East India Company armies, attracted by immediate promotion by one rank; their new brevet ranks brought higher pay, provided by the British authorities. During the

FAR LEFT
Bashi-bazouk of Beatson's Horse; Maj Beatson recruited up to 1,000 each of Anatolians, Syrians, Albanians/Bosnians, and Macedonians. This irregular cavalryman wears his own clothing, and carries the usual pistols and bladed weapons thrust under his sash.

LEFT
An Arab *bashi-bazouk* of the Crimean War, dressed all in crimson with lavish gold embroidery. He might well be a member of the *Spahis d'Orient* raised by the French expeditionary force. This corps was commanded by Gen 'Youssouf', born Joseph Vantini, a Corsican enslaved as a boy by Tunisian pirates and converted to Islam. He later rose through the ranks in the French *Chasseurs d'Afrique* and *Spahis Algériens* in North Africa.

war the 17,000 men of the Anglo–Turkish Contingent mostly performed auxiliary duties, such as garrisoning important locations, before the corps was finally disbanded in May 1856.

Attached to the ATC was another 'independent' regular unit of Turkish soldiers, led by 12 British officers who were mostly promoted ex-NCOs. Created by Maj Beatson, and surviving the disbandment of his cavalry corps, this Osmanli Horse Artillery consisted of four mounted troops, with 9-pdr guns and 24-pdr howitzers.

Polish volunteers

Polish nationhood had been destroyed by the Third Partition (1794–97) between Russia, Austria and Prussia, and Napoleon's revived Grand Duchy of Warsaw had lasted only from 1807 to 1815. Thousands of Poles had fled abroad, and many more following the failure of the 1830–31 November Uprising against Russia. Significant numbers subsequently entered the service of the Ottoman Empire, happy to fight Russia at any opportunity. With British and French sponsorship, Poles who had crossed the borders into Ottoman territory south of the Danube had even established a sort of logistical base known as the 'Eastern Agency'.

During the last months of 1853 one Polish expatriate, Michal Czajkowski (later known as 'Sadik Pasha'), was tasked by the Turkish authorities to raise a new Cossack regiment from any Slavic Christians living inside the Empire, and from Cossacks in northern Dobruja on the west coast of the Black Sea, as the embryo for a planned 'Christian Army' in Ottoman service. Czajkowski's 1st Cossack Regt had five regular squadrons of lancers and one of Cossack irregulars (two more incomplete Cossack squadrons were added later). The unit was given elegant uniforms and the old banner of the Zaporozhian Cossacks; against all expectations, it fought well on several occasions, helping to offset Russian superiority in light cavalry. A 2nd Cossack Regt, initially known as

British officer of the Osmanli Horse Artillery. His striking uniform consists of a red helmet with a falling red plume, brass fittings and chinscales; a dark blue patrol jacket with gold collar embroidery, frontal frogging, and Hungarian knots on the sleeves; and dark blue trousers with red side-stripes.

the 'Polish Legion', was formed in 1854 by Count Wladyslaw Zamoyski, and a 3rd during 1855. However, the latter two units failed to match the quality of the first, and both were disbanded after a few months. In autumn 1855 all the Polish cavalry serving in the Ottoman army were reorganized as a 2,000-man 'Cossack Brigade'; largely equipped and paid for by the British and French, this never saw combat, and was disbanded in July 1856.

During 1856, for just a few months, the British and French organized a 4,000-strong 'Cossack Division' of their own from Polish exiles. This consisted of one line infantry regiment, one of light infantry, a regiment of lancers and one of mounted carabiniers, and one battery each of foot and mounted artillery. After the end of the Crimean War this formation was disbanded, never having seen active service.

In 1857, during the reorganization of the Ottoman army following the end of the Crimean War, the Turks decided to re-raise their Cossack Bde under command of Sadik Pasha. The reconstituted corps consisted of two 4-squadron regiments: the Cossack Regt and the Dragoon Regt, which were both given Guard status. During 1857–65 the brigade was mostly employed to patrol the border with Greece and to fight local brigands. In 1865 the Dragoon Regt was disbanded and the Cossack Bde ceased to exist; the Cossack Regt was retained as part of the Imperial Guard, until it was destroyed early in the Russo–Turkish War (1877–78).

In 1876, shortly before the outbreak of that war, the Ottomans raised a new but very small 'Polish Legion'. During the war it served in two separate detachments, each of an infantry company and a cavalry squadron, in the Balkans and the Caucasus; both were disbanded at the end of the war.

THE RUSSO–TURKISH WAR, 1877–78

Summary

Sultan Abdulmejid I was succeeded by Abdulaziz (r. 1861–76), who concentrated on strengthening the Ottoman Navy, and who also recognized Ismail Pasha, *vali* (governor) of Egypt, as the *khedive* (viceroy). Abdulaziz's successor, Murad V, was physically and mentally incapable, so was deposed after less than a year in favour of his half-brother Abdul Hamid II (r. 1876–1909). It was he who was obliged to resist Russia's fifth attack on the Ottoman Empire since 1800. (For a full account, and many more uniform illustrations, see MAA 277 *The Russo–Turkish War 1877*.)

In barest summary, Russia – impelled by a pan-Slavic movement seeking the liberation of Christian peoples in the Turkish-ruled Balkans, and exploiting international outrage over reports of atrocities by Turkish irregulars in Bulgaria – declared war in April 1877. The Tsar sent major forces south across the Danube, and, while diversionary operations took place in the Caucasus, the war in the Balkans centred on attempts to

Lebanese militiamen photographed in *c.*1860. At least two are armed with double-barrelled hunting shotguns, and three carry very broad-bladed sabres slung at the hip as well as pistols and daggers in their sashes. Both Druze and Christian communities in the Levant raised militias, but they were usually too busy fighting each other to be of much value to the Ottoman government.

take heavily fortified places protected by large Ottoman forces. Atrocities were committed against civilians by both sides.

In most actions neither side showed much tactical talent, usually employing unimaginative frontal attacks, though an exception was Prince Imeretinski's impressive victory at Lovtcha in early September. Osman Pasha's army successfully held Plevna against three assaults on 26 and 30 July and 11 September, but it fell on 10 December after a five-month siege. Suleiman Pasha was badly defeated at the Shipka Pass on 21–25 August and again on 17–18 September. The Russians pushed across the Balkan mountains despite harsh winter weather; Sofia fell on 4 January 1878, and Suleiman Pasha was routed in Thrace later that month. This left Istanbul naked, except for the protection of a British naval squadron – once again, the Great Powers were determined to shape and balance the peace settlement, which eventually robbed Russia of much of its gains.

Military Service Law, 1869

Following the Crimean War, the Ottoman army drew heavily upon contemporary French examples, but little improvement was achieved during the 1860s. In 1869 a new Military Service Law was promulgated, which extended conscripts' theoretical liability for service to 20 years. It did this by creating two new military structures: a first-line reserve of the active regular army (the *Ihtiyat*), and a territorial militia (the *Saliss,* soon redesignated the *Mustahfiz*). Each Turkish conscript, selected at the age of 20, was to serve for 4 years in the regular *Nizam-i Cedit,* and then for 2 years in the new *Ihtiyat* reserve. After these first 6 years he joined the *Redif* second-line reserve for 6 years, and subsequently passed into the *Mustahfiz* for 8 years. This new territorial militia existed on paper only, comprising able-bodied men aged 32 to 40 who could be mobilized only in case of foreign invasion. Those conscripts who were not initially drafted for service in the *Nizam-i Cedit* had to serve in the *Redif* for an increased period of 9 years.

The army officer corps was also reorganized, being divided between two main categories. The first comprised those who were commissioned

19

upon graduating from one of the military academies, and the second those who were promoted from the ranks after passing an examination. In addition to the already existing military colleges, two more were created: the Pancaldi school for infantry and cavalry officers, and the Halidji-Oglow for artillery and engineer officers. Upon leaving active service, most officers continued their military careers in the *Ihtiyat* and subsequently *Redif* reserves.

The new service law allowed the creation of a 7th Army Corps, based in Yemen. At the same time the Gendarmerie, which now consisted of both infantry and cavalry, was reorganized in eight autonomous regiments.

The Ottoman Army, 1877

In 1877 the *Nizam-i Cedit* consisted of the following formations and units:

1st Army Corps (Istanbul): 2 regiments of Guard infantry, 5 regiments of line infantry, 7 battalions of light infantry; 2 regiments of Guard cavalry, 3 regiments of line cavalry; 1 regiment of active artillery, 1 regiment of reserve artillery (12 field batteries and 1 mountain battery); 1 brigade of engineers with 4 battalions (each with 2 companies of engineers, 1 company of sappers and 1 company of artificers).

2nd Army Corps (Danube): 7 line inf regts, 6 light inf bns; 4 line cav regts; 1 regt of active artillery, and 1 sapper company.

3rd Army Corps (Bulgaria): 11 line inf regts, 9 light inf bns; 4 line cav regts; 1 regt of active artillery, 3 btys of reserve artillery (mountain guns), and 1 sapper company.

4th Army Corps (Anatolia): 6 line inf regts, 6 light inf bns; 3 line cav regts; 1 regt of active artillery, and 1 sapper company.

5th Army Corps (Syria): 7 line inf regts, 7 light inf bns; 4 line cav regts, 1 camel corps with 6 sqns; 1 regt of active artillery, and 1 sapper company.

6th Army Corps (Baghdad): 6 line inf regts, 6 light inf bns; 2 line cav regts; 1 regt of active artillery.

7th Army Corps (Yemen): 5 line inf regts, 5 light inf bns; 1 regt of active artillery.

The regiments of Guard and line infantry had three 8-company battalions each, and the light infantry battalions were of the same size. Several line regiments and light battalions were designated 'frontier infantry', but apart from this title they did not differ from the norm; three regiments and two battalions of such 'frontier infantry' in 3rd Army Corps were entirely recruited from Bosnians. The Guard and line cavalry regiments each had 6 squadrons. Each regiment of active artillery was to have 9 field and 3 mounted batteries, each with 6 pieces, but there were some exceptions: some regiments included batteries of mountain guns or machine guns. Except for a few units listed above under army

This illustrates the major Ottoman trend towards French uniform styles between the Crimean and Franco-Prussian Wars (1856-1870); see commentary to Plate E1. The NCO (left) and private of the Imperial Guard's 1st Zouave Regt wear the M1861 uniform. The NCO is distinguished by the more extensive red embroidery on his dark blue bolero jacket, while the inverted red chevron on his upper left sleeve indicates his length of service. Both figures have red trousers and white spat gaiters; the NCO is wearing a dark grey hooded cloak, while the private has a green regimental turban.

corps, the reserve artillery units of the *Ihtiyat* were autonomous: 1 field regiment, 7 garrison regiments, and 2 separate garrison battalions with three batteries each.

Second-line reserves and auxiliaries

Additionally, the *Redif*, at least on paper, could muster 240 infantry battalions, but the *Mustahfiz* did not have a stable structure. Neither the *Redif* nor the *Mustahfiz* now provided any cavalry, so to supplement the regular regiments the authorities had begun from 1861 to raise some squadrons of irregular 'volunteer' cavalry from suitable ethnic groups. A Circassian and a Kazakh squadron were the first, soon followed by others mainly recruited from Kurdish and Arab communities, and by 1877 some 50 squadrons had been formed.

From 1861 the Ottoman authorities also tried to 'regularize' the many *bashi-bazouks* who were still part of the potential military forces. Attempts were made to provide some sort of uniform, and to introduce Turkish regular officers. Each autonomous band was now to be commanded by a *bimbashi* (major), and was to be organized in autonomous companies each led by a *yuzbashi* (captain) and *mulazim-i evvel* (lieutenant), while company NCOs were to be chosen from the most experienced fighters. Despite these efforts, however, the *bashi-bazouks* performed very badly during the Russo–Turkish War, and the great majority of units were permanently disbanded at the end of hostilities.

An excellent print illustrating *bashi-bazouks* in Ottoman service during the Russo–Turkish War. The peculiar tall headgear and complex decorative costume identify them as the famous *zeybeks*, irregular fighters recruited along the Aegean coastline of Anatolia. Note the long flintlock muskets with several barrel-bands and prominent butt decoration, and the usual arsenal of sidearms, which in their case included *yataghan* sabres.

THE LATE OTTOMAN ARMY

Military Service Law, 1879

After the end of the Russo–Turkish War, Sultan Abdul Hamid II again had to reform his defeated *Nizam-i-Cedit*, and in 1879 a new Military Service Law adjusted the terms of service. Conscripts would henceforth serve for 3 years in the active army and then 3 years in the *Ihtiyat* first reserve; they would then pass into the *Redif* second reserve for 8 years, and subsequently into the *Mustahfiz* militia for 6 years. Only Christians continued to be exempted from compulsory military service. Following this reform both the *Ihtiyat* and the *Redif* became more effective; until 1879 the former had provided only a few units of reserve artillery, and the latter a certain number of poorly-trained infantry battalions.

The new conscription system eased the army's manpower shortage, but did little to improve its overall quality. The Empire now took the victorious Prussian army as its model, and in 1882 the sultan invited a German military mission to Istanbul. This remained active until the outbreak of World War I, and would play a significant role in the political activity that culminated in the 'Young Turks' revolution in 1908. The army's overall organization in seven army corps was retained, but within

ABOVE LEFT
NCO of the 4th Cavalry Regt from 1st Army Corps, wearing M1879/93 dress with a black *kalpak.* The dark blue single-breasted tunic has the collar, straight cuffs and frontal piping in the regiment's green distinctive colour, and brass *contre-epaulettes.* The inverted chevrons of rank are red, and the side-stripes on his light blue trousers are green. See also commentary to Plate G3.

ABOVE RIGHT
Exemplifying the varied appearance of the multi-ethnic Ottoman forces, these members of the irregular *Hamidiye* corps, photographed in 1895, wear traditional Circassian-style dress; see also Plate G3.

them divisions and brigades began to be assembled. Each army corps was to have the following active formations:

Two line infantry divisions, each with two 2-regiment brigades and one rifle battalion.

One cavalry division with three 2-regiment brigades (one active, and two *Ihtiyat).*

One active artillery regiment with 14 batteries (9 of field artillery, grouped in three battalions; 3 of mounted artillery, in 1 battalion; 1 of mountain artillery, and 1 equipped with Gatling machine guns produced on license in Austria).

One reserve/garrison artillery regiment.

Each army corps could also call upon four 2-brigade infantry divisions from the *Redif,* and two 2-brigade divisions from the *Mustahfiz.*

A line infantry regiment had four battalions, plus a squad of sappers, while a cavalry regiment had five squadrons. The engineers were organized in four regiments, which were not integral to the army corps. A single regiment of reserve field artillery was stationed in Istanbul.

Abdul Hamid II also reorganized his Imperial Guard, developing it to include the following: 8 regiments of infantry, 2 regiments of Zouaves (light infantry); 3 regiments of cavalry plus 1 elite lancer regiment; and 1 brigade of mounted artillery. The infantry regiments doubled as the 2 divisions of the 1st Army Corps, but the two 2-battalion Zouave regiments had a particular character: their 1st Regt was made up of Albanian volunteers, and the 2nd of Tripolitanian volunteers from Libya. The sultan probably formed these units (which received elegant uniforms) to attract young volunteers from two regions where the conscription system was not working well. Two of the Imperial

Guard's cavalry regiments doubled as the active brigade of the 1st Army Corps' cavalry division, while the third was titled the *Ertugrul* Regiment. The brigade of 'mounted' artillery actually had one field battery and two mounted batteries. Abdul Hamid II also improved the training of the single naval infantry battalion, and created an independent regiment of Gendarmerie for the city of Istanbul.

Hamidye irregulars, 1890s

The new system of recruitment introduced in 1879 never did work properly, since some entire eastern and southern ethnic groups failed to contribute conscripts as they should have done. In 1891 an attempt began to regularize the many squadrons of 'volunteer cavalry' that had existed for a generation. The authorities decided to create a new corps of semi-regulars known as *Hamidye* (literally 'belonging to Hamid', i.e. the sultan). Modelled on the Russian Cossacks, these came to comprise 57 regiments, provided by 65 different tribes of the Empire's Circassian, Turkomen, Kurdish and Arab ethnic minorities. Each regiment usually had 3 companies of light cavalry and 2 of light infantry, but there were exceptions. Initially the *Hamidye* units were to be deployed in the Caucasus region to defend against Russian attacks, but the Ottomans soon started to encourage them to harass the large Armenian communities living in the eastern part of the Empire. The *Hamidye* had no military training or discipline to speak of, but were extremely loyal to the sultan; the privileges they enjoyed included a degree of legal impunity for crimes committed against other ethnic groups.

Further 1890s reforms

In 1893 two 'special military districts' were created in addition to the seven army corps: that of Tripolitania (western Libya) and Hijaz (western Arabia). Each was garrisoned by one newly-formed 'independent division' of the Ottoman Army. That in Tripolitania consisted of 4 line infantry regiments and 1 light battalion; 1 cavalry regiment; and 1 artillery battalion (with 2 field, 2 fortress and 1 mountain battery). The Hijaz division had only 3 line infantry regiments, and 1 artillery battalion (with 2 field and 2 fortress batteries).

Also during 1893, some well-organized militia corps were created in a few frontier regions of the Empire. In Tripolitania, the independent regular division was supported by 30 infantry battalions and 60 cavalry squadrons. In Lebanon, 2 infantry battalions and a cavalry detachment were recruited from both Christians and Druzes. In Kurdistan, 24 five-squadron cavalry regiments were raised, and in Yemen, 4 four-company infantry battalions to act as a local gendarmerie.

In 1897, on the renewal of hostilities with Greece over Crete, the Ottoman authorities authorized the creation of yet another category of 'auxiliary' irregular troops: the *Ilave*. This consisted of temporary infantry battalions, similar to the former *bashi-bazouks*, which

Tripolitanian soldiers of the Imperial Guard's 2nd Regt of Zouaves in 1890, wearing M1879 uniform. Dark blue with red edging and embroidery, this was practically identical to the M1861 uniform for line infantry (Plate E1); the embroidery on the chest of the bolero jacket is just visible at left and centre. For more details see commentary to Plate G1.

were supposed to be armed only for the duration of a war.

In 1899, a new conscription law divided new recruits into two categories: the *tertib-i evvel,* who were required to serve full time, and the *tertib-i saani,* who served in the active army only for 6–9 months in any single year. For the former, service was for 3 years in the active army and the next 3 in the first reserve. Upon reaching 27 years of age a conscript passed into the *Redif* for 8 years (during which he usually spent only one month in every 2 years under arms). Finally, he passed into the *Mustahfiz* for 8 years. This new system was not applied in Tripolitania or Hijaz, and Christians and the inhabitants of Istanbul and the cities of Mecca, Medina and Jeddah were all exempt from compulsory service.

Ottoman troops marching off for the First Balkan War in 1912. Some wear artillery knee-boots, but in this high-contrast photo it is hard to tell if they wear the new khaki M1909 uniform, old M1879/93 dark blue, or a mixture of both. Most wear loose turbans, but there is at least one early example of the *kabalak* or 'Enver hat'. (Private collection)

THE 'YOUNG TURKS' REVOLUTION

The army in 1909–14

From 1908, following this complete upheaval of the Ottoman government, the army began to undergo structural reorganizations, though these took some time to be achieved.

First, the large Imperial Guard forged by Abdul Hamid II was disbanded, and replaced with just two small ceremonial units. One was a single company of foot Palace Guards, formed from the former Halberdiers, and the other a single squadron of Mounted Bodyguards, formed from selected members of the former *Ertugrul* Regiment. The Istanbul gendarmerie regiment was retained, however. During 1908 the *Hamidiye* tribal regiments were also disbanded. In July 1909 the new Turkish parliament finally extended military conscription to

Photographed in 1912, this bearded line cavalryman wears M1909 khaki uniform. His turban is very loosely wrapped around the frame of his *kabalak,* making it almost unidentifiable. His belt pouches are of German design, matching his Mauser rifle. (Private collection)

24

(continued on page 33)

A

VASSAL STATES, 1835–52
1: Serbia: Private, Line Inf Bn, 1842
2: Moldavia: Trooper, Lancer Sqn, 1843
3: Wallachia: Private, 1st Bn Frontier Lt Inf, 1852

B

CRIMEAN WAR, 1853–56
1: Private, 1st Inf Regt, Ottoman 2nd Army Corps, 1853
2: Trooper, Mounted Chasseurs, 2nd Army Corps, 1854
3: Tunisia: Trooper, Cavalry Regiment, 1856

C

CRIMEAN WAR, 1853–56
1: Quartermaster, 7th Inf Regt, Anglo–Turkish Contingent, 1855
2: Major, Beatson's Horse, 1854
3: Lancer, 1st Cossack Regt, 1853

D

INTER-WAR YEARS, 1857–76
1: Ottoman private, 1st Bn Foot Chasseurs, 1861
2: Montenegro: Guardsman, Guard of the Prince, 1858
3: Egypt: Guardsman, Khedive's Life Guards, 1863

E

RUSSO–TURKISH WAR, 1877–78
1: Lt, 1st Cav Regt, Ottoman Imperial Guard, 1877
2: Egypt: Private, 1st Line Inf Regt, 1877
3: Ottoman *bashi-bazouk*, 1878

F

OTTOMAN ARMY, 1879–98

1: Private, 1st Regt of Zouaves, Imperial Guard, 1898
2: Gunner, 1st (Mtd) Bn, 1st Regt of Field Artillery, 1885
3: Divisional general, *Hamidiye* corps, 1893

UNDER THE 'YOUNG TURKS', 1899–1914
1: Private, Ottoman *Redif* infantry, 1912
2: Crete: Lance-corporal, Gendarmerie, 1899
3: Macedonia: *Ilave* irregular, 1908

H

Troops marching through Istanbul in 1912, giving a clear impression of the M1909 khaki uniform, worn with a *kalpak* of brown false lambswool. The varying shades of tunics and trousers are presumably due to dispersed manufacture. (Private collection)

the Christian subjects of the Empire for the first time. In 1910 the Ottoman army consisted of the following units:

75 four-battalion active line infantry regiments, and 18 four-battalion light infantry regiments; 95 *Redif* reserve regiments of line infantry; 300 *Mustahfiz* militia battalions; and 666 *Ilave* battalions of irregular light infantry.

38 five-squadron active line cavalry regiments; 12 four-squadron *Redif* reserve cavalry regiments.

35 regiments of field artillery; 2 regiments of heavy artillery (howitzers); and 145 companies of fortress artillery.

7 four-company battalions of engineers; 7 independent companies of radio-telegraphists; and 7 three-company 'train' (i.e. transport) battalions. Each army corps had one battalion of engineers, one company of radio-telegraphists, and one train battalion.

Gendarmerie: 30 regiments, totalling about 450 foot companies and 100 mounted squadrons.

In January 1914 yet another new conscription law was promulgated, making a conscript liable to serve for 25 years in total: 2 years in the active army, 18 in the reserve (the *Ihtiyat* and *Redif* being merged together), then 5 years in the *Mustahfiz*. The old structure of seven army corps was replaced with a new divisional system within the four military districts that remained after the great territorial losses in the Balkan Wars:

1st Military District (remaining European territory in Thrace, and western Anatolia): 5 army corps each having 3 divisions.

2nd Military District (Syria): 2 army corps each having 3 divisions.

3rd Military District (Kurdistan, and eastern Anatolia): 3 army corps each having 3 divisions.

Ottoman artillery in Tripoli, western Libya, in 1911–12. The uniforms are M1909, the weapons Krupp 7.5cm field guns, of which the Ottoman army had acquired more than 730 of various models during the first decade of the 20th century. (Private collection)

4th Military District (Mesopotamia): 2 army corps each having 2 divisions.

In addition to these there were three 'special military regions' in Arabia: Hijaz and Dawasir, each with 1 division, and Yemen with 2 divisions.

An Ottoman division consisted of three 3-battalion infantry regiments, plus between 6 and 9 field or mountain artillery batteries. Attached to each army corps were a 2-regiment cavalry brigade (each regiment having 5 squadrons); 3 independent howitzer batteries; a battalion of engineers; a battalion of the train; and a company of radio-telegraphists.

ARMIES OF VASSAL STATES

Egyptian army, 1815–82

The army of Muhammad Ali initially consisted of Albanian Muslim *arnaut* mercenaries, and a certain number of Mameluke heavy cavalry who joined his service after their caste had been largely defeated by the French. After first fighting the Wahhabis in Arabia on behalf of the Ottomans, Muhammad Ali tried to 'westernize' his Albanian soldiers, but he was resisted by their traditionalist leaders, who mutinied in 1815. In 1820 he tried to organize some 1,300 black Sudanese prisoners into a modernized force by hiring French officers and Greek NCOs. When this attempt failed, in 1822–24 Muhammad Ali introduced a ruthless programme of conscripting local Egyptian *fellahin* peasants for a new army, and in 1824 a French military mission led by Gen Pierre Boyer arrived to supervise organization and training. Given 'westernized' uniforms and French M1777 muskets, about 17,000 infantry organized in four regiments were sent to Greece to fight the local rebellions against the Ottomans, supported by some cavalry and artillery.

By 1831, the army was well-trained and well-organized, and structured in the following units: 1 Guard infantry regiment, and 14 line regiments; 1 Guard cavalry (cuirassier) regiment, and 4 line regiments; 1 artillery regiment; 2 engineer battalions and a company of artificers; and a company of gendarmerie. The infantry regiments had 4 battalions each, organized on the French pattern with 6 fusilier companies and 1 each of grenadiers and voltigeurs. The cavalry regiments had 4 squadrons, each of 4 troops. The artillery regiment had 6 batteries, equipped with modern pieces brought by the French military mission.

In order to meet his manpower needs, Muhammad Ali was soon forced to introduce conscription for a period of 12 years' military service, though the inhabitants of Alexandria, Cairo and Suez were exempted. By the end of 1837, after further expansion, the army of Muhammad Ali's son Ibrahim Pasha consisted of the following: 3 Guard infantry regiments, and 31 of the line; 2 Guard cavalry regiments, plus 2 mounted bodyguard companies, and 13 line cavalry regiments; 1 Guard artillery battalion, 4 regiments of line foot artillery, and 2 mounted regiments; 1 battalion and 2 companies of sappers; 2 battalions of the train; plus 2 regiments and 3 battalions of veterans (garrison infantry). These regular troops were supported by several thousand *bashi-bazouks*, mostly Arab *bedouin*.

After the 'stolen' war of 1839–41 with the Ottoman Empire, the Egyptian army was greatly reduced and most of its Guard corps were disbanded. By the outbreak of the Crimean War in 1854 it comprised the following: 20 line infantry regiments; 1 regiment of Guard cavalry (cuirassiers), and 10 regiments of line cavalry (lancers); 3 artillery regiments; and 2 battalions of engineers. Of these, Muhammad Ali's grandson Abbas Pasha sent the following units to fight against Russia in 1854: 9 line infantry regiments; a squadron of Guard cavalry and 2 line regiments; and one-and-a-half artillery regiments. Men of this force are recorded as fighting in the successful defences of Silistria on the Balkan front in May-June 1854, and of Eupatoria in Crimea in February 1855.

Egyptian army, 1838: gunners and officer (right) of Guard artillery. All wear the red cap with black tassel; the gunners' red single-breasted jackets bear gold chest loops and embroidery, including on the upper sleeves, and the baggy red trousers have gold embroidery around the side pockets. The officer has tasselled gold frogging on his chest and more elaborate embroidery on the upper sleeves and forearms. He wears a black crossbelt with gilt fittings, a gold waist-sash, and apparently gold cords-and-flounders at his right breast. The gun is a French 12-pdr Gribeauval field piece.

Egyptian army, c.1860: trooper of 3rd (Hussar) Sqn, Khedive's Life Guards in M1859 dress – see also commentary to Plate E3. The black busby has a red top bag, and yellow cords with tasselled flounders. The iron-grey dolman has a red collar and pointed cuffs piped in yellow, and yellow frontal frogging; the waist-sash is red and yellow. The red pelisse has yellow frogging and black fur edging; the trousers are white and the boots black. Note the interesting carbine with a pistol-grip and 'frame' butt.

During 1856–70 the army was in decline, but it did send a single battalion to Mexico in 1863 to support Napoleon III's expeditionary army. In 1859 the Guard cavalry regiment had been reorganized as the 'Khedive's Life Guards', with one squadron each of mounted grenadiers, lancers, and hussars; from 1863 all three were uniformed and equipped as hussars. In 1877 the Egyptian line comprised 18 infantry regiments (2 of them entirely recruited in Sudan); 4 light infantry battalions; 4 cavalry regiments; 4 field artillery regiments, and 3 of fortress artillery; and 3 engineer battalions. An infantry regiment had three 8-company battalions, and light infantry battalions were the same size. A cavalry regiment had 3 squadrons equipped with lances and 3 with carbines. A field artillery regiment had three 4-battery detachments (2 mounted detachments and one foot). The engineer battalions had 8 sapper and 2 pontoon companies.

By 1870 military schools for the officers of each branch had been created. Active service for conscripts had been reduced to 5 years, plus 7 years in an 'army of the reserve' (which was organized only with difficulty). The 8,000-odd Egyptian troops which participated in the Russo–Turkish War (1877–78) consisted of 12 line infantry battalions and one field battery. In 1882, following the so-called 'Anglo-Egyptian War', Egypt ceased to be a vassal of the Ottoman Empire and became a British protectorate.

Tunisian army, 1830–81

The Ottoman governors of Tunis had had a few Janissaries from the Balkans or Anatolia, but otherwise relied upon irregular tribal cavalry. The first military reforms began during the last months of 1830, following the French conquest of Algiers, when the ruler Hussein Bey feared an imminent French expansion. By 1832 he had two 2-battalion line infantry regiments , and a third was raised in 1837, but an attempt to introduce conscription failed completely. In 1838 a cavalry lancer regiment and an artillery regiment were formed. In 1840 a military school was established at Bardo; in 1842 another three infantry regiments were raised from conscripts; and in 1846 a second artillery regiment was created. From 1843 a French military mission was active in Tunisia, but its instructors had little success; the recruiting system remained haphazard, with conscripts called up only when some new corps was being raised.

By 1847 the Tunisian army consisted of: a small mounted 'Bey's Bodyguard'; 7 regiments of line infantry, each of 3 battalions with 8 companies, and a regiment of naval infantry; 1 cavalry regiment with 4 squadrons; 2 regiments of artillery, organized like the infantry units; 3 corps of *Spahis* irregular cavalry, and several auxiliary foot units recruited from the warlike Zwawa tribes. During 1848–53 another two regiments of artillery were formed, and the regiments of infantry and artillery began to be termed 'brigades' despite retaining their internal organization.

The Tunisian expeditionary force sent to take part to the Crimean War consisted of 7,000 men, in 6 infantry battalions, 1 cavalry regiment, and two 6-gun field batteries. Tunisian troops are recorded at Batoum during the Caucasus campaign. In 1860 the army was reduced to 6 regiments of infantry, a squadron of cavalry, and a regiment of artillery. During that same year a new conscription law required selected recruits to serve for a period of 8 years. In 1881, shortly before France's conquest of Tunisia, the army comprised 7 infantry regiments, a cavalry squadron, and 4 artillery battalions.

Serbian army, 1808–76

Historically, in the western Balkans the Serbs and the Bosnians had strong militias; the Serbian *hayduks* were Christians, while the Bosnian *pandours* were Muslims. Having a long military frontier with the Austrians, the overstretched Ottoman authorities had been obliged to permit their Serbian and Bosnian subjects to carry weapons as a matter of course. Since the middle of the 18th century a new class of local 'frontier soldiers' had emerged in both regions for guerrilla border operations; organized in 100-strong companies, both the *hayduks* and the *pandours* were extremely mobile and flexible.

The first 'regular' Serbian troops – one regiment each of infantry and cavalry – were organized in 1808, from among the insurgents fighting the Ottomans during the First Serbian Uprising. These two units, uniformed and equipped by the Russians, were disbanded in 1813 when the uprising was crushed.

In 1830, following the Ottoman defeat in the Russo–Turkish war of 1828–29, the Principality of Serbia was permitted to have a small regular army. As in 1808–13, this was organized and trained by Russian instructors. Initially it had just one 4-company line infantry battalion, one cavalry squadron, and one battery of field artillery. Although designated as a fusilier unit, the infantry battalion had a light infantry character; the cavalry squadron was equipped and dressed similarly to contemporary Russian Cossacks. The officers, sent to Russia, soon acquired thorough training.

In 1847 a 2nd Inf Bn was raised, and the cavalry squadron were transformed into *uhlan* lancers. In 1850 an artillery school was founded, which later became Serbia's first general military academy. Following the end of the Crimean War the Serbian army came under increasing French influence, and started to improve its standards. In 1859 a new 'Mounted Bodyguard of the Prince' squadron was created, equipped and uniformed as hussars. In 1863 a small engineer corps was formed, as well as a train corps as part of the artillery.

By 1876, shortly before the outbreak of the Russo–Turkish War that won Serbia's independence, the military forces consisted of the following: 2 line infantry battalions, each with 4 fusilier and 1 each grenadier and voltigeur companies; 2 cavalry squadrons (one each Guard and line); 12 artillery batteries (8 field and 4 mountain); and 2 engineer battalions. These corps were supported by a highly-militarized gendarmerie, as well as by a 'reserve army', and a general militia that could be mobilized in emergencies.

Montenegrin army, 1830–76

The first regular military unit of the Principality of Montenegro was created during 1830–31: a small *gvardija* (guard company) with 156 men, tasked with keeping order among local communities as a sort of gendarmerie. In 1837 this was expanded to 400 men, and began to receive regular pay from the Ottoman central government. In 1852, after Montenegro became a largely-autonomous vassal state, the territory of the princedom was divided into 40 (increased to 50 in 1858) administrative units known

Egyptian army, *c*.1863: line infantryman of the Sudanese battalion sent to accompany the French expeditionary army in Mexico. His red *fez* has a black tassel, his lightweight jacket and trousers are entirely white, and the waist-sash is red. The tan leather *jambières* and white spats are French army issue.

Tunisian army, 1831 (left to right, foreground): senior officer of artillery, junior officer, line infantryman, and cavalryman. For colours, see commentary to Plate C3. The artillery officer has an embroidered gold branch badge on his *tarboosh*; both officers display gold piping to their red collars, gold epaulettes of rank, and gilt gorgets.

as 'captaincies'; each of these was to provide one 100-man company of semi-permanent soldiers, commanded by a captain. In 1852 Prince Danilo of Montenegro also organized his own personal guard; this was initially 400 strong, but was increased to 1,000 in 1858 when the old *gvardija* was disbanded. The Guard of the Prince was itself disbanded in 1863.

Three years later, the first group of young Montenegrin officers began their training by a small military mission sent by Serbia. In 1871 the Montenegrin army received a new structure, which remained unchanged until the princedom started the 1876 conflict that would win it independence. This new organization consisted of the following: 6 battalions of Guard infantry; 23 battalions of line infantry; and one battery of mountain artillery. All the Montenegrin footsoldiers were equipped as light infantrymen, and did not wear 'westernized' uniforms. Each battalion of line infantry was recruited from two or three local communities, while the Guard infantry were selected from among the best soldiers throughout the country.

Moldavian army, 1830–59

In the north-eastern Balkans, the autonomous 'Danubian Principalities' of Moldavia and Wallachia had historically maintained local forces. These were a mix of local levies and foreign mercenaries, who served under local nobles as well as under the Greek Phanariote governors appointed by the Ottomans. The militiamen were known as *slujitori* in Moldavia and as *dorobanti* in Wallachia.

The Moldavian army was created in 1830, following the Russo–Turkish war of 1828–29. Heavily influenced by Russian practice, it always

remained quite a small force. Initially it consisted of just one 4-company line infantry battalion, and one cavalry squadron of lancers. In 1845 a 2nd Inf Bn was formed, and the two units were assembled as a regiment; in the same year a second lancer squadron was also raised. In 1848 the line infantry was expanded with a 3rd Bn, and all three formed a single 'Regiment of Musketeers'. Two years later the two existing cavalry squadrons were merged into a 'Regiment of Lancers'.

In 1851 the first artillery field battery was created. In 1856 an independent battalion of light infantry (*vanatori*) was raised, and, following its success, in 1858 another two were formed and the three units were consolidated into a 'Regiment of Chasseurs'. In 1857 a second battery of field artillery was organized, followed by a single battalion of engineers early in 1859.

In addition to this small standing army, the Principality of Moldavia also had three locally-recruited paramilitary police corps: the *Slujitori de granita* (Frontier Policemen), the *Slujitori de ocoale* (District Policemen), and the *Jandarmii* (Gendarmes) The Frontier Police were organized in 1852, having 400 infantrymen and 100 cavalrymen distributed among 19 frontier posts. The District Police dated from 1830, and in 1852 were organized in 8-man detachments, one for each of the Moldavian districts. The Gendarmerie, including both foot and mounted gendarmes, were created in 1852, and consisted of 14 companies. The capital of Moldavia, Iasi, also had an autonomous foot company and a mounted squadron of *Jandarmii*.

Wallachian army, 1830–59

Like that of Moldavia, the Wallachian army was also formed in 1830, as a consequence of Russia's victory in 1828; it too was strongly influenced by Russia, and of fairly modest size.

Initially it consisted of 6 line infantry battalions each of 4 companies, and 6 squadrons of lancers. In 1834 the foot battalions were consolidated

into three 2-battalion regiments, and the lancer squadrons were attached in pairs to these new foot regiments. In 1843 the lancer squadrons were detached from the infantry, their number being reduced from six to three; during that same year a single battery of field artillery was created. In 1849 Wallachia's strength was increased by the formation of a new paramilitary corps, the *Graniceri* (Frontier Light Infantry). This was organized in two autonomous 'inspectorates'; the first, tasked with guarding the Danube frontier, had three 4-company battalions, while the second, with two battalions, guarded the frontier running across the Carpathian Mountains. During 1849 the Wallachian artillery consisted of one field battery and a mounted half-battery. In 1852 the three lancer squadrons were reduced to two, which in 1856 were assembled to form a regiment.

In addition to its standing army, the Principality of Wallachia also had a locally-recruited paramilitary police corps: the *Dorobantzi* (Mounted Gendarmes), who received a proper organization in 1850. They numbered a total of 17 squadrons, which were divided between two inspectorates to cover Oltenia or Western Wallachia and Muntenia or Eastern Wallachia.

In 1859 the Wallachian army was merged with that of Moldavia following the unification of the two Danubian Principalities under a single prince. This gave birth to an independent nation: from 1862 the Romanian United Provinces, and from 1866 the Kingdom of Romania.

SELECT BIBLIOGRAPHY

anonymous, *Observations on the Turkish Contingent* (Smith, 1856)

Babac, Dusan, *The Serbian Army in the Wars for Independence against Turkey 1876-1878* (Helion & Company, 2015)

Cooke, W.S., *The Ottoman Empire and its Tributary States* (Clowes and Son, 1876)

Drury, Ian, *The Russo–Turkish War 1877,* MAA 277 (Osprey Publishing, 1994)

Esposito, Gabriele, *Armies of the Italian-Turkish War 1911–1912,* MAA 534 (Osprey Publishing, 2020)

Fahmy, Khaled, *All the Pasha's Men: Mehmed Ali, his army and the making of modern Egypt* (University of Cairo Press, 2002)

Flaherty, Chris, *The Ottoman Imperial Army in the First World War: a Handbook of Uniforms* (Partizan Press, 2014)

Flaherty, Chris, *Turkish Crimean War Uniforms* (self-published, 2020)

Jovic, T. & Jovicevic, M., *The Montenegrin Army: Organization and Uniforms* (Nasljede, 2006)

Jowett, Philip S., *Armies of the Balkan Wars 1912–1913*, MAA 466 (Osprey Publishing, 2011)

Jowett, Philip S., *Armies of the Greek-Turkish War 1919–1922*, MAA 501 (Osprey Publishing, 2015)

Lamouche, Léon, *L'organisation militaire de l'Empire Ottoman* (Librairie Militaire de L. Baudoin, 1895)

Muzeul Militar National, *Armata Romana in vremea lui Alexandru Ioan Cuza 1859-1866* (Total Publishing, 2003)

Muzeul Militar National, *Uniformele Armatei Romane 1830–1930* (Marvan, 1930)

Nicolle, David, *Armies of the Ottoman Empire 1775–1820*, MAA 314 (Osprey Publishing, 1998)

Nicolle, David, *Lawrence and the Arab Revolts*, MAA 208 (Osprey Publishing, 1989)

Nicolle, David, *The Ottoman Army 1914–1918*, MAA 269 (Osprey Publishing, 1994)

Roubicek, Marcel, *Early Modern Arab Armies* (Franciscan Press, 1977)

Roubicek, Marcel, *Modern Ottoman Troops 1797–1915 in Contemporary Pictures* (Franciscan Press, 1978)

Uyar, M. & Erickson, E.J., *A Military History of the Ottomans* (Praeger, 2009)

Vasic, Pavle, *Uniforms of the Serbian Army 1808–1918* (Prosveta, 1980)

Vladescu, Cristian M., *Uniformele Armatei Romane* (Editura Meridiane, 1977)

Wallachian army, 1843: artillerymen – see commentary to Plate B3. The new *pickelhaube* was black with brass fittings and front plate, and a black falling plume. The dark blue single-breasted tunic had a black collar and cuffs, red cuff flaps, and red piping to the facings and front edge; the dark blue trousers had red side-stripes.

PLATE COMMENTARIES

Uniforms and equipment

A: *NIZAM-I CEDIT* & EGYPT, 1797–1834
A1: Fusilier, 1st Infantry Regiment, 1807
The infantry of the New Army that existed before 1807 were dressed quite similarly to the old *Bostanci* of the Imperial Guard, red being the latter's distinctive colour until 1839. The units were distinguished by the facing colour of the collar and cuffs. The 2nd Inf Regt, having a distinctly 'provincial' character, was the only unit to wear a dark blue jacket instead of red. The regimental 'cannon infantry', existing until 1836, wore a distinctive uniform consisting of a tall black hat trimmed with fur around the base, a dark blue jacket and loose trousers.

In 1826 the new regular infantry received short single-breasted jackets in regimental colours, and grey trousers for all units, The headgear was a *tarboosh* with a rounded crown profile, in regimental colours decorated with yellow tape stripes. The Guard infantry had red jackets, and the tall red headgear of the *Bostanci*, shown in Plate A2. The artillery wore a tall red *fez*, a dark blue jacket with a red crescent on the chest, and loose grey trousers. The *Humbaraci Ocagi (*Regt of Bombardiers) had a notably tall black cylindrical hat, brown jacket and grey trousers, though

Trooper of the Ottoman Imperial Guard's 3rd Cavalry Sqn in 1828 uniform; compare with Plate A2. He wears a tall red *Bostanci* cap with yellow stripes, a dark green jacket with tasselled red frogging and a silver crescent badge, dark blue trousers and black boots. The 3rd Sqn differed from the other two in being equipped with carbines rather than lances, though all had saddle pistols.

its Polish members were permitted to wear a black *czapka* with a brass crescent on the front. The naval infantry wore a red *fez* with dark blue tassel, a red jacket with two rows of tasselled silver 'buttonhole loops' on the chest, and loose red trousers.

In 1832 new uniforms were introduced for both the artillery and the naval infantry. The former now had a red *fez* with dark blue tassel, dark blue jacket with yellow collar and cuff embroidery, and loose grey trousers; the latter had the same *fez* and trousers but a red jacket. The standard weapon during this early period was the French M1777 flintlock musket, but apparently the 'Brown Bess' was also seen in great numbers.

A2: Lancer, 1st Cavalry Squadron, Imperial Guard, 1828
The 1st and 2nd Sqns of the Guard cavalry wore the uniform illustrated; the 3rd Sqn had dark green jackets with red frogging, and dark blue trousers with red embroidery. The line cavalry, organized from 1828, wore the same basic uniform as here, but with jackets of regimental colours and universal grey trousers without embroidery. The Silistra Cav Regt was initially uniformed in light green, but changed to light blue when it became the Sesiasker Regiment.

In 1832 the cavalry uniform became a red *fez* with dark blue tassel, a single-breasted jacket in regimental colours (see below) with red piping to collar and cuffs and five red 'loops' across the chest, and loose trousers in regimental colour (dark green, brown, dark blue and light blue for the 1st–4th Regts respectively).

A3: Egypt: Cuirassier, Guard Cavalry Regiment, 1831
The Egyptian army started to receive uniforms during the years 1822–24. Those of the infantry were very simple: a red *fez* with black tassel, a dark blue single-breasted jacket with collar and pointed cuffs in regimental colours, and baggy dark blue trousers. The Guard infantry, organized in 1831, was dressed like the line but with red jackets and trousers, the former having five gold-lace 'loops' across the chest. The *zirkhagi* or 'iron men' of the Guard cavalry used this helmet and cuirass.

The line cavalry were uniformed like the line infantry, but with five 'loops' of regimentally-coloured lace across the chest. The Guard artillery were dressed in red, the line artillery in dark blue. During the hottest months all units wore white linen jackets and loose trousers. From about 1841 a red standing collar and frontal lapels were ordered added to line infantry jackets, but these were never popular, and were not worn by the Egyptian contingent to the Crimean War.

B: VASSAL STATES, 1835–52
B1: Serbia: Private, Line Infantry Battalion, 1842
The Serbian regular infantry of 1808 were issued a black shako bearing a cockade in the national colours, a dark green double-breasted coatee with red facings and white shoulder straps, and white trousers. The regular cavalry had a black fur 'busby' with a red top 'bag' and white plume, a dark green single-breasted jacket with straight red cuffs, and white trousers.

In 1830 the new Serbian regular infantry were uniformed in a medium-blue *tarboosh* cap with yellow edging and black leather visor, a dark green coatee with red collar and cuffs, and medium blue trousers with red side-stripes. The cavalry busby then had a red plume topped with medium blue; a dark brown single-breasted jacket had red facings, and medium-blue trousers had red side-stripes. In 1837 the infantry uniform changed to a green shako with silver-coloured frontal plate bearing Serbia's coat-of-arms, and a white-and-red pompon; a green single-breasted coatee with red straight cuffs and frontal piping; and green trousers with red side-stripes. The cavalry busby had a plume in national colours; their dark blue dolman jacket had yellow frontal frogging and red facings piped in yellow, and their light blue trousers had red side-stripes.

In 1841 new dress regulations prescribed the infantry uniform illustrated here. For parade the soft fatigue cap was replaced with a black shako having a silver frontal plate and red-and-green pompon. The cavalry received a black shako with a silver plate and red pompon; a dark blue *kurtka* jacket with red frontal plastron and facings decorated with white braid; and dark blue trousers with red double side-stripes. In 1847 the infantry and artillery would receive a new Prussian-style uniform: a black *pickelhaube* helmet with brass frontal plate and fittings; a dark blue single-breasted tunic with red cuff flaps and edging and piping to the facings; and dark blue trousers with red side-stripes. The cavalry exchanged their shako for a white *czapka* with a red plume, and started to wear grey trousers on campaign. The Mounted Bodyguard of the Prince, created in 1859, kept the black busby with red bag; their medium-green dolman had gold frogging, and their red trousers gold side-stripes.

In 1861 new French-style uniforms would come into use, with a forward-slanting *képi,* double-breasted tunic and grey trousers. The *képi* and tunic were dark green for the infantry, light blue for the cavalry, and dark blue for the artillery; the facings of the tunic and the trouser side-stripes were red. In 1870 a new and very modern campaign dress would appear: a light blue-grey fatigue cap; a dark brown single-breasted four-pocket tunic, with collar patches in branch-of-service colours; and light blue trousers with red side-stripes.

B2: Moldavia: Trooper, Lancer Squadron, 1843

The Moldavian army of 1830 wore a black busby with a red bag and brass frontal plate; a dark blue single-breasted coat with collar and straight cuffs piped in red; and dark blue trousers with red side-stripes. In 1835 the busby was replaced with a black shako, and the cavalry received light blue trousers.

In 1843 the cavalry changed to the new Polish-style uniform shown here. In 1845 the infantry were given grey trousers, and a taller model of shako with black pompon, but in 1847 they were ordered into a new Prussian-style uniform. The black *pickelhaube* had a brass frontal plate and fittings; the dark blue single-breasted tunic had a red collar and cuff flaps, and grey trousers had red side-stripes (replaced with white trousers in summer). The artillery were dressed like the infantry, but with black collar and cuffs. The *Slujitori* were dressed like the soldiers of the regular army, but with a black tunic.

B3: Wallachia: 1st Battalion of Frontier Light Infantry, 1852

The Wallachian army formed in 1830 wore a black busby with a yellow bag and a brass frontal plate; a dark blue single-breasted coat with yellow collar and straight cuffs; and dark blue trousers with yellow side-stripes. In 1837 the infantry's

Standard-bearer of the Ottoman 1st Cossack Regt in 1854; for colours, compare with Plate D3. Note the double-sleeved coat, with a pair of slit outer sleeves worn thrown back from the shoulders. The flag of the Zaporozhian Cossacks was red, with a white cross on one side and a white Archangel Michael on the other.

busby was replaced with a black shako , and the coat collar received white braid bars.

In 1843 the infantry received a new Prussian-style dress similar to the Moldavian uniform described under B2. The artillery were dressed like the infantry, but with black collar and cuffs. The *Graniceri* wore this practical brown campaign uniform, with minimal dark green facings; the *Dorobantzi* were dressed in dark grey with green facings. and wore the fur-trimmed *papacha* headgear of the contemporary Caucasian Cossacks, also with a green bag.

C: CRIMEAN WAR, 1853–56

C1: Private, 1st Infantry Regiment, Ottoman 2nd Army Corps, 1853

In 1839 the Ottoman line infantry abandoned its previous 'semi-traditional' dress, and received a dark blue European-style 'shell jacket' piped with red around the

Egypt: troopers of the 1st (Horse Grenadier) Sqn and 2nd (Lancer) Sqn of the Khedive's Life Guards wearing 1859 uniform; compare with Plate E3, showing the hussar uniform extended in 1863 from the 3rd Sqn to the whole unit. (Horse grenadier, left): black bearskin with white plume, cord and flounders; iron-grey tunic with green collar and edging to pointed cuffs, white tape 'loops' across chest and white epaulettes; green-and-white waist-sash, baggy white trousers and black boots. (Lancer, right): white metal dragoon helmet with brass plate and comb, red tuft and black horsetail; iron-grey tunic with red collar and edging to pointed cuffs, white 'loops' and epaulettes; red-and-white sash, trousers and boots as 1st Squadron.

collar and straight cuffs. This was worn with the usual red *fez* having a dark blue tassel, and with grey or white (summer) trousers. The Guard infantry were distinguished by red facings, and three tasselled red 'loops' across the chest. Naval infantry uniforms resembled those of the line, but in medium blue and with brass *contre-epaulettes* on the shoulders.

In 1853, shortly before the outbreak of the Crimean War, this new French-style uniform, with a long single-breasted tunic piped red on the collar, front, cuffs and cuff-flaps, was ordered for the line infantry, and for the light infantry but with green distinctions. The Ottoman artillery and the naval infantry retained their M1832 and M1839 dress respectively. The engineers wore a red soft cap similar to that of Plate A1, together with a long dark blue frock coat with red facings, and red trousers. The Gendarmes were dressed like the line infantry but with iron-grey tunics and trousers. By 1853 a good number of the Ottoman army's French and British Napoleonic-era muskets had already been converted to the percussion system (like that shown here), but many soldiers continued to carry old flintlocks. Only the light infantry could count on a certain number of M1851 Minié rifle-muskets imported from France.

C2: Trooper, Mounted Chasseurs Regiment, Ottoman 2nd Army Corps, 1854

The line cavalry – except for the Mounted Chasseurs, who wore the uniform illustrated here – had dolman jackets in regimental colours, with yellow frogging and piping; the *fez* was red and the trousers were white. The Guard cavalry, since 1840, were dressed in hussar style but with the red *fez* with dark blue tassel; their dolmans (red for the 1st Regt and blue for the 2nd) bore gold frogging and piping, and all wore white trousers. The Guard's elite 1st Regt of Lancers were uniformed in Polish style: same headgear as the other Guard cavalry, but dark blue *kurtka* with red frontal plastron and facings piped in white, and dark blue trousers with red double side-stripes.

C3: Tunisia: Trooper, Cavalry Regiment, 1856

The Tunisian contingent that participated in the Crimean War was still dressed in the uniform introduced in 1830–31, the cavalry unit as illustrated here; white jackets and trousers were in common use during hot weather. The infantry wore this same red *tarboosh* with black tassel, a dark blue single-breasted jacket with red collar and straight cuffs, and plain dark blue trousers. The artillery were uniformed similarly, but with a yellow flaming shell embroidered on the front of the headgear, where the naval infantry displayed an embroidered yellow anchor.

In 1881, shortly before being disbanded by the invading French, the Tunisian army adopted new uniforms modelled on those of France's *Armée d'Afrique*. All branches wore a red *chéchia* with black tassel; a dark blue bolero jacket with red embroidery and trim including piping to the pointed cuffs; a dark blue vest with red trim; a red waist-sash, and loose white trousers.

D: CRIMEAN WAR, 1853–56

D1: Quartermaster, 7th Infantry Regiment, Anglo–Turkish Contingent, 1855

The soldiers of the Anglo–Turkish Contingent's 16 regiments were dressed like Ottoman line infantrymen, but with tunic cuffs in distinctive colours assigned by their British instructors. The British officers and NCOs of the corps were uniformed like this figure, with dark blue or red-peaked forage caps displaying a brass crescent on the front, and dark blue shell jackets. These bore the badge of the ATC, comprising Queen Victoria's monogram, on the right forearm above the rank chevrons.

D2: Major, Beatson's Horse, 1854
Beatson's British officers wore this simple uniform resembling that of the contemporary native cavalry of the East India Company's armies, with an emerald-green *kurta* blouse. The *bashi-bazouks* of the *Spahis d'Orient* and of Beatson's Horse (later known as the Osmanli Irregular Cavalry) wore the traditional clothing of their ethnic groups.

The gunners of the Osmanli Horse Artillery were dressed like their Ottoman counterparts, but their officers had a very elegant uniform: a spiked red helmet with brass chinscales and red falling plume; a dark blue patrol jacket with red collar and pointed cuffs piped in gold, and gold frontal frogging and 'Hungarian' sleeve-knots; and dark blue trousers with red side-stripes (see page 18).

D3: Lancer, 1st Cossack Regiment, 1853
The Cossack units of the Ottoman Army that were active during the Crimean War wore the Polish-style uniform illustrated here (see page 43).

The new Cossack Regt later organized in 1857 received the following uniform: a *papacha* trimmed with brown fur, displaying a brass crescent on the front; a dark blue double-breasted, long-skirted tunic with red frontal edge-piping, red collar and straight cuffs piped in white, and white *contre-epaulettes;* and dark blue trousers with red side-stripes. In 1861 the headgear became a black busby with a red top bag and white pompon; the tunic was exchanged for a single-breasted jacket of the same colours; and the trousers became entirely white. The Polish Dragoon Regt which existed until 1865 was dressed like the standard Ottoman line cavalry. The Polish Legion of 1876 was dressed like the rest of the Ottoman army, but with a red *czapka* headgear trimmed in white.

E: INTER-WAR YEARS, 1857–76
E1: Private, 1st Battalion of Foot Chasseurs, Ottoman Army, 1861
During the Crimean War the Ottoman military authorities were greatly impressed by the appearance of Napoleon III's *Armée d'Afrique,* and in 1861 they issued new dress regulations that prescribed French-style 'Zouave' uniforms for most Ottoman units. The light infantry wore the uniform shown here, with green trim and embroidery, while the line infantry had these features in red. The two regiments of Guard infantry also received Zouave dress, the 1st and 2nd Regts with red and yellow distinctions respectively; they also wore turbans wrapped around the *fez*, in light green and white respectively. The M1861 uniforms for the artillery and naval infantry were both almost identical to those of the line infantry. During the hottest months all foot troops replaced their Zouave uniforms with an entirely white smock that was pleated at the front, worn with white trousers. In 1861 the Gendarmerie also received new Zouave-style dress, entirely in light blue with yellow embroidery and trim.

By the end of the Crimean War, thanks to major purchases of weapons from their allies, the Ottomans had entirely replaced their old Napoleonic muskets with new French M1851 Minié and British M1853 Enfield rifles. During the

1900: Ottoman horse artillerymen serving an M1881 Krupp 7.5cm field gun; for M1879/93 uniform, see Plate G2.

1860s the latter were gradually exchanged for M1866 British Snider-Enfields, and by the outbreak of the 1877–78 Russo–Turkish War most of the regular infantry had replaced the latter with the M1871 Martini–Peabody, which was acquired in large numbers. By 1877 the Ottoman cavalry had replaced its old percussion carbines with M1873 Winchesters, while the artillery had substituted Krupp field guns and Gatling machine guns for its Napoleonic-era smoothbores.

E2: Montenegro: Guardsman, Guard of the Prince, 1858
The Montenegrin army never had proper uniforms during this period, and its members wore the traditional civilian clothing of their communities. Only officers, from 1854, were required to wear a gold badge on the front of their headgear in order to be recognizable. Until 1871 most Montenegrin soldiers continued to be equipped with a bewildering variety of old-fashioned Balkan weapons including flintlock hunting guns, flintlock pistols, and daggers. From 1871 a certain number of modern rifles started to be imported from the Austro-Hungarian Empire.

E3: Egypt: Guardsman, Khedive's Life Guards, 1863
From 1859 the three squadrons of the Khedive's Life Guards were given particular uniforms; see captions on pages 36 and 44 for more details. In 1863 they all received the hussar-style dress shown here, which had been used by the line cavalry since 1859, but without the pelisse and with loose white trousers.

In 1859 the Egyptian line infantry replaced its old uniforms with simpler and more practical alternatives: a red *chéchia* with black tassel, a dark blue single-breasted jacket with red standing collar and straight cuffs (entirely white during the hottest months), and loose white trousers. The artillery were uniformed similarly.

F: RUSSO–TURKISH WAR, 1877–78
F1: Lieutenant, 1st Cavalry Regiment, Ottoman Imperial Guard, 1877
In 1861 the cavalry of the 1st Army Corps were given Zouave-style uniforms; these had the bolero in red for the Guard regiments and in dark blue for the other units (the Guard's elite separate 1st Lancer Regt retained its Polish-style dress). The line cavalry of the other army corps were issued a new uniform that was clearly influenced by that of the 1st

Drummer (left) and bugler (right) of the Ottoman light infantry in M1879/93 uniform; compare with Plate H1 for basic colours, but here the facings and piping are green instead of red. The drummer has the same brown leather apron as used by sappers.

Cossack Regt (see Plate D3). This consisted of a black lambswool *kalpak* cap with a red top; a dark blue double-sleeved, single-breasted coat worn over a short red single-breasted jacket; and light blue trousers with red side-stripes. The collar and pointed cuffs of the coat were in different regimental colours, following the same sequence within each army corps: first regiment, red collar and cuffs; second, red collar and white cuffs; third, red collar and crimson cuffs; and fourth, red collar and green cuffs. The 'volunteer' cavalry units raised since 1861 were mostly dressed like the later *Hamidiye* corps (see Plate G3).

F2: Egypt: Private, 1st Line Infantry Regiment, 1877
The M1859 uniforms of the Egyptian army remained in use until 1882; they were only partly modified in 1871, when white piping was added to the line infantry's jacket, its collar and cuffs became dark blue, and dark blue trousers with white side-stripes were introduced. In that same year, following the French practice that had been seen by the Egyptian contingent during the 'Mexican Adventure', red inverted chevrons began to be worn to indicate completed years of service (though in the Egyptian case, above the cuffs). During hot weather an entirely white uniform was worn. The light infantry were dressed like the line, but in light blue. The artillery were also uniformed like the line infantry, and cavalry uniforms did not change after 1863. The Egyptian army replaced its old Charleville or 'Brown Bess' flintlocks with M1851 Minié rifles; these, in turn, were replaced in 1871 with the M1867 Remington 'rolling block' rifle shown here.

F3: *Bashi-bazouk*, Ottoman army, 1878
The irregular *bashi-bazouks* continued to wear colourful civilian clothing until their final virtual disappearance after this war. Their costumes usually included striped turbans, highly-ornamented jackets, silk waistcoats and multi-coloured waist-sashes, loose trousers, and pointed shoes made of painted leather. In 1861 the Ottoman authorities tried to introduce a uniform costume, as illustrated here, to all the bands of *bashi-bazouks,* but this experiment was a complete failure, since the great majority of the irregulars ignored it.

G: OTTOMAN ARMY, 1879–98
G1: Private, 1st Regiment of Zouaves, Imperial Guard, 1898
In 1879, soon after the end of the Russo–Turkish War, new dress regulations were usually but not invariably influenced by contemporary Prussian military fashion. These remained in force until 1908, although slightly modified in 1893. Under the 1879 regulations, the 1st Regiment of Zouaves of the Imperial Guard was to wear the white uniform illustrated here, while the 2nd Regt was to be uniformed like the pre-1879 line infantry. The other foot regiments of the Guard and the line were to be dressed like Plate H1. The newly-created sappers of the foot units had a black apron in the Imperial Guard, and a brown apron in the line infantry. The light infantry was dressed like the line, but with facings and piping in green rather than red. The officers' uniforms basically resembled those of the rankers, but with double-breasted tunics having Prussian-style gold cord shoulder straps showing their rank.

G2: Gunner, 1st (Mounted) Battalion, 1st Regiment of Field Artillery, 1885
According to the 1879/93 dress regulations, the Ottoman foot artillery were dressed like the line infantry. The horse artillery, as here, wore a black fleece *kalpak* and a dark blue tunic with black dolman-syle frogging between three rows of buttons.
The Gendarmerie were uniformed like the mounted artillery, but with gold piping to the collar and cuffs; in 1903 the colour of the officers' dolman was changed to light blue. The engineers were dressed like the foot artillery, but with light blue facings and piping. The ratings and NCOs of the naval infantry were given dark blue 'sailor jackets' with two rows of front buttons, and white trousers; their officers were uniformed like their line infantry equivalents, but with gold cuff-ring ranking instead of shoulder straps.

G3: Divisional general, *Hamidiye* corps, 1893
The *Hamidiye* wore the uniform shown here, which was very similar to that of the contemporary Russian Cossacks, and included several elements derived from Circassian traditional costume.
The M1879 uniform for the line cavalry consisted of a black *kalpak;* a dark blue single-breasted tunic with collar, straight cuffs and frontal piping in regimental colours (unchanged from the previous dress regulations), dark blue collar patches with brass unit numbers, and brass *contre-epaulettes;* and light blue trousers with side-stripes in regimental colours. The elite 1st Regt of Lancers had a black *kalpak;* a dark blue tunic with red frontal plastron, red collar and pointed cuffs adorned with white lace, and red-and-white *contre-epaulettes;* and dark blue trousers with red side-stripes. The *Ertugrul* Regt wore a black *kalpak*, dark green double-breasted tunic with red frontal piping, red collar and pointed cuffs adorned with white lace, and white *contre-epaulettes;* and dark green trousers with red side-stripes.

H: UNDER THE 'YOUNG TURKS', 1899–1914

H1: Private, Ottoman *Redif* infantry, 1912

In 1908, soon after the 'Young Turks' took power, the Ottoman army issued its first experimental khaki-brown uniform to the 1st Bn of Engineers for field trials. The results were positive, and in 1909 the new uniform was authorized for the whole army. However, only the active units were completely re-uniformed, and many soldiers of the *Redif* – like this man – fought in the Balkan Wars still wearing their old dark blue M1879/93 dress.

We have chosen not to illustrate here the M1909 uniform (which can be seen in a couple of the accompanying photographs, and on Plate F of MAA 534, *Armies of the Italian-Turkish War*). The new khaki-brown tunic had a folded collar, five frontal buttons for rankers and NCOs and six for officers. Rankers and NCOs had four-pocket tunics; those of officers were privately tailored, often in Germany, so varied – most showed only external flaps for internal skirt pockets, but some had four pockets. Officers' tunics had the collar entirely faced in distinctive branch colours: olive-green for infantry, light-grey for cavalry, and dark blue for artillery; NCOs wore only patches of these colours on their khaki collars. Officers' rank was shown by five-point stars pinned to Prussian-style bullion cord shoulder straps, while NCOs had simple cloth sleeve-stripes.The uniform included puttees and shoes, but the cavalry and artillery wore black kneeboots instead. The new standard headgear was a *kalpak* made from brown artificial lambswool, shaped like a *fez* but without a tassel. The officers' *kalpak* was of black real lambswool with a branch-colour top, crossed by three lines of gold lace superimposed to divide it into six segments.

During 1912 Enver Pasha, then one of the Ottoman officers fighting against the Italians in Libya, created a new kind of headgear specifically for desert combat. This *kabalak* consisted of a long piece of white or khaki cloth wrapped around a wickerwork frame, and served as a sun-helmet. The *kabalak* began to be worn by other Turkish officers in North Africa; it was steadily adopted throughout the whole Ottoman army from the First Balkan War onwards, and was the norm (at least in Anatolian units) during World War I.

Following the adoption of the new M1909 uniforms, the two small remaining units of the Imperial Guard were the only Ottoman corps to be dressed in colourful uniforms. The Palace Guard wore a red-topped white *kalpak* with a brass frontal badge; a red single-breasted tunic with white piping to the collar and pointed cuffs, white lace on the cuffs, white fringed epaulettes, and white *aiguillettes* on the right shoulder; and red trousers with broad white side-stripes. The Mounted Bodyguards had an all-black *kalpak* with a brass badge; a light blue dolman with double sleeves, black frontal frogging and Hungarian sleeve-knots, and brass *contre-epaulettes;* a red single-breasted jacket with black-piped pointed cuffs, worn under the dolman; and red trousers with black side-stripes.

H2: Crete: Lance-corporal, Gendarmerie, 1899

Crete was given autonomous vassal status after the Greco-Turkish war of 1897, and retained it until 1908. During this period it had an independent 1,600-strong gendarmerie, trained and commanded by instructors from the Italian *Carabinieri,* and forming one 5-company battalion.The uniform, designed by one of its Italian instructors, had some elements in common with that of the *Carabinieri,* such as the

black colour and the silver lace bars on the collar, while the black *kalpak* and loose trousers show clear Ottoman influence. The weapons carried by this policeman are also Italian: an M1891 Carcano rifle and M1889 Bodeo revolver.

The new corps of gendarmerie or militia that were organized in some regions of the Ottoman Empire from 1893 mostly wore the traditional civilian clothing of their communities; but an exception was the Lebanese militia, who were given old M1861 Zouave-style uniforms – probably surplus holdings from military stores.

H3: Macedonia: *Ilave* irregular, 1908

The *Ilave* irregulars, like the Macedonian illustrated here, wore no uniforms and were dressed in their national clothing. They were mostly equipped with old M1871 Martini-Peabody rifles, which were replaced in the regular army with M1898 Mausers from 1903.

Ottoman sentry during the 1913 Second Balkan War; he wears dishevelled M1909 khaki uniform, again with an untidily wrapped *kabalak* headgear. (Private collection)

INDEX

Page locators in bold refer to plate captions, pictures and illustrations.

Abdul Hamid II, Sultan 18, 22–23
Abdulaziz, Sultan 18
Abdulmejid I, Sultan 13
Alemdar Mustafa Pasha 6
Ali, Muhammad 7–8, 10, 34–35
Anglo-Egyptian War 36
Anglo-Turkish Contingent 16–17, **D1** (44)
arnauts, Albanian 5, 7, **9**, 12
artillery 5, **6**, 11, 13, **15**, **33**, **35**, 41, **G2** (46)
   Humbaraci Ocagi 11
   Osmanli Horse Artillery 17
   Suratçi Ocagi 5
   Topçu Ocagi **6**
'Auspicious Incident' 10
azaps, Anatolian 5

bashi-bazouk mercenaries 13, 15–16, **17**, 21, **21**, **F3** (46)
Beatson's Horse 16, **16**, **17**, **D2** (45)
bin Saud, Abdullah 7
Bostanci musketeer regiment 6, **10**
Bostansyan-i Hassa infantry regiments **6**, 7, 10–11
Bucharest, Treaty of 7

categories of troops, 18th-century 5
cavalry 13, 14, **15**
   Osmanli Irregular Cavalry 16
   Polish 17–18
   Sesiasker (Silistra) Regiment 11
   Sipahis 5, 10
colleges, military 14, 20
conscription 13, 14, 21–22, 24, 33
Cossack Regiment 18, 43, **D3** (45)
Cretan gendarmerie **H2** (47)
Crimean War 1853–56 14–18, **C1** (44), **C2** (44), **C3** (44)
Czajkowski, Michal (Sadik Pasha) 17

Danubian Principalities 3–4, 7, 14
Delis irregulars 5

Edirne incident 6
Egypt 7
Egyptian army 34–36, **35**, **37**, **A3** (42), **F2** (46)
   Khedive's Life Guards 36, **36**, **44**, **E3** (45)
Ertugrul Regiment 24

fusiliers **11**

Gendarmerie 14, 24, **H2** (47)
Greece 3, 7

Hamidiye corps **22**, 23, 24, **G3** (46)
hayduk militia 37

headgear
   Bostanci cap 42, **A1** (42)
   busby **39**, **B3** (43)
   cap 6, **10**, **11**, **12**
   chéchia **E3** (45)
   czapka 43
   fez **9**, **13**
   kabalak **24**, **34**, **47**, **H1** (47)
   kalpak **22**, **33**, **F1** (46), **G2** (46)
   pickelhaube 40, **B2** (43)
   shako **40**, **B1** (43)
   tarboosh **10**, **A1** (42)
   turban 6, **16**, **20**
   see also uniforms

Ihtiyat reserve 19, 21
Ilave auxiliaries 23, **H3** (47)
Imperial Guard 13, **13**, **20**, 22, **23**, 24, **42**, **A2** (42), **F1** (45)
   see also Zouaves

Janissaries 5, 10

Kars, siege of 15

Lebanon 5, **19**

Mahmud II, Sultan 7, 10, 13
Mamelukes 4, **5**
mercenaries 5
Mesopotamia 5
Mexico 36
Military Service Law 1869: 19–20
Miners, Regiment of 11
Moldavia 4
Moldavian army 38–39, **39**, **40**, **B2** (43)
Montenegrin army 37–38, **E2** (45)
Montenegro 3
Murad V, Sultan 18
musicians 14, **46**
Mustafa IV, Sultan 6–7
Mustahfiz militia 19, 21

Napoleonic Wars 7
naval infantry 14
Nizam-i Cedit (New Army) **6**, 6–11, 20–22, **A1** (42), **A2** (42), **E1** (45)
   see also under individual arms

Omar Pasha 14–15
Osmanli Horse Artillery 17, **18**, 45
Ottoman Empire 3, **4**, 8–9

Palestine 5
pandour militia 37
Polish troops 17–18

ranks 10–11
Redif reserve 3, 12, 14, 19, 21, **H1** (47)
reforms, 1890s 23–24

Romania 40
Russo-Turkish War 1877–78: 18–21, **F1** (45)

Saliss militia 19
Selim III, Sultan 6
Serbia 3, 6, 7
Serbian army 37, **39**, **B1** (42–43)
seshaneci rifles 13
Shemshi Pasha *see* Beatson's Horse
Spahis d'Orient 16, **17**
stratkulu troops 5

Tanzimat (Reorganization) 1840–53 13–14
tertib-i evvel conscripts 24
tertib-i saani conscripts 24
toprakh troops 5, 6
Tunisian army 36–37, **38**, **C3** (44)

uniforms
   cloak **20**
   fustanella kilt **9**, **12**
   gaiters **20**
   kurtka jacket 43
   leggings **9**
   M1826 **10**
   M1839 **13**
   M1859 **36**, **F2** (46)
   M1879/93 **3**, **22**, **23**, **45**, **46**, **H1** (47)
   M1909 **24**, **33**, **34**, **47**
   sash **6**
   shoes **13**
   trousers **6**, **13**, **15**, **20**, **35**
   see also headgear

Wahhabis, Arabian 7, 10
Wallachia 4
Wallachian army 39–40, **40**, **41**, **B3** (43–44)
weapons
   artillery **6**, **33**, **35**, **41**
   carbine **36**
   curved dagger **5**
   hunting gun **12**, **19**
   lance **5**, **44**, **C3** (44)
   machine gun **34**
   musket 11, **21**, **C1** (44), **F3** (46)
   pistol **5**, **6**, **19**
   rifle **D1** (44), **E1** (45), **E2** (45), **F2** (46), **H1** (47), **H2** (47), **H3** (47)
   sabre **5**, **19**, **21**, **D2** (45), **G3** (46)

yamak auxiliaries 5
Young Turks Revolution 24, 33
Youssouf, General 16, 17

zaptiye 14
zeybek irregulars **21**
Zouaves 20, 22–23, 45, **G1** (46)
   see also Imperial Guard